- the -
ADDICTION
FORMULA

A holistic approach to writing captivating, memorable hit songs. With 317 proven commercial techniques and 331 examples.

Written by Friedemann Findeisen

ISBN: 978-90-823913-0-5

Published in 2015 by Albino Publishing
Albino Publishing
Hendrik ter Kuilestraat 140
7547 BE Enschede
Netherlands

http://holistic-songwriting.com

Book design by Friedemann Findeisen

TESTIMONIALS

"Friedemann strikes completely new paths by throwing music, arrangement, lyrics and production into the storytelling pot. Forget yesterday's songwriting and all idols you're trying to imitate. This book describes a new, up & coming, not yet conceivable, maybe not even born generation of songwriters"

Marc David (Kolibeat)

"Wow, I can't believe someone actually found a holistic approach to songwriting that explains how arrangement, production, lyrics, melody, harmony, rhythm, etc. work together in a hit song"

Thomas Muis (Composer)

"Fresh and easy-to-read. Mr. Findeisen makes his case not by rehashing (often) "dry" theory, but by providing clear visual and linguistic examples that speak most effectively to 21st Century songwriters (along with plenty of references to recent hit songs)"

Tom Salisbury (Grammy-Award Winning Arranger)

"[This book] completely changed the way I listen to composition and analyse arrangements. Friedemann explains his theories clearly, in-depth and with a great sense of humor. A must-read for every songwriter and conservatory student"

Frederike Berendsen (Singer/Songwriter)

"A revelation for songwriters who feel rightly overwhelmed or wrongly underwhelmed by how well-crafted hit-songs truly are. [This book] explains the techniques behind the great pop songs with great humor, clarity and tons of visual and auditory examples. Expect lots of "aha!" moments and the understanding that songwriting is not as difficult as it seems, just hard work. Once you know the rules, the fun really begins and this book lays them out in the clearest way possible"

Benjamin Samama (Topline Writer, Berklee Teacher)

"This book reveals the secrets to hit songwriting in a logical and unique way. While most books give you rules that can always be broken, this book goes for the root of the problem and shows you how to write songs on the highest level. This is the new way of encoding hit songwriting"

Jobassa (Performing Artist)

"Today's biggest bands and artists all have something in common and Friedemann unravels this secret in his own, fascinating way. He combines storytelling in movies with lyric writing and song build. The analysing goes deep and the tools are useful and inspiring. Highly recommended."

Erwin Steijlen (Pink, Shakira)

If You Only Have **2 Minutes**

Are you in a book store and the owner is really uptight about reading too long in the same book? Or are you reading this page online and you just want to know the basics of the Addiction Formula? Then this page is for you.

The Addiction Formula is designed to captivate your audience and guide their attention through your songs. With the techniques outlined in this book you will be able to turn any song into an audience magnet that is extremely compelling to listen to and hard to turn off.

To accomplish this, we will borrow psychological principles from addiction (as in drug abuse, binge-watching *Lost* or eating Twinkies) to structure our song, set energy levels and transition between sections.

The three tools that will help us with this are hype (relative energy), tension (gradual energy) and implied tension (superimposed energy). Once you understand these simple tools, driving attention will become second nature to you. After a little while, using the formula will be easy and fun.

If you have 5 more minutes, read on…

If You Only Have **5 Minutes**

It seems the staff of your book store is friendly. Or you're really pushing your luck. Either way, let's get into a little more detail.

So we've already talked about structuring in a compelling way (what I call Lyric-Less Storytelling). In the Addiction Formula, we use energy curves to represent our story. It visualizes structure, arrangement and many other things at a glance. You can see such an energy curve on the next page.

I'm sure you've already used this particular structure (verse, chorus, verse, chorus, bridge, chorus). And if you haven't used it, you have heard it at least a couple thousand times on the radio.

In part 1 of this book, we'll go into why this and other structures work better than others and how they trigger certain things in your brain when you hear them.

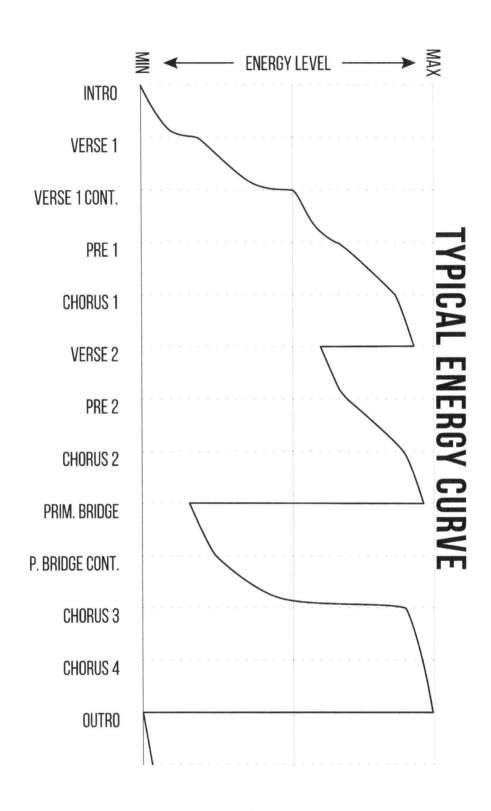

This stuff is gold if you want to know how to captivate an audience at the deepest level. And if that's not enough for you, I'll even teach you four simple steps to create your own, unique energy curves.

In part 2, we move from framework to practice. These chapters are all about translating your curve into music. We will go into detail as to how you can increase or decrease the energy and how to build up to certain moments. This part of the book is similar to an encyclopaedia with lists of techniques you can use in any song.

Part 3 then is about putting all you have learned together. Here, we will go through the 10 steps of the Addiction Formula and see where we can go from there. We will also do something that no other songwriting book has ever done before: Give you the tools to create your own techniques. This might be the most valuable part of this book if you are seeking to sound more unique and stand out from the crowd.

Naturally, I don't expect you to believe a single word I say without proof, so every technique or idea in this book comes with examples from the billboard charts of the past 25 years. We are talking modern songwriting here - no examples that are older than this allowed!

Do you need to know music theory? While some theory knowledge can help you with this book, it isn't all that necessary. We're writing for non-musicians, not for music teachers or musicologists. You will notice upon flicking through this book that I don't use notation or any other conventional way of describing music. Am I saying music theory is outdated? No. But there are plenty of hit songwriters out there who can't read music and in order to understand the Addiction Formula you don't need to either.

If this is where you put the book back onto the store's shelf, let me thank you for reading this far. I hope the few points I could share with you will make a difference. Good luck!

If however you want to dive in deep and learn about all of the nuances that make this approach work, read on.

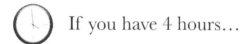 If you have 4 hours…

CONTENTS

PREFACE

Story Is Dead, Long Live Story.

As far as I'm concerned, storytelling in music is about over. Yes, it still pops up every now and then in some country songs or your latest folk hit, but overall, songwriters are moving away from telling fully fleshed-out stories through their songs.

This in turn means one very important aspect of songwriting just falls by the wayside: dramaturgy. What storytelling did for centuries (going all the way back to bards) is provide a reason for listening to the whole song: If you wanna know what happens to Georgie, you have to keep listening[1]. Every songwriter knows: Give the audience a good story and they'll stick around[2].

Now look at the following songs:
Sam Smith - *Stay With Me*,
Katy Perry - *I Kissed A Girl*,

---

1 Rod Stewart - *The Killing Of Georgie*

2 The Beatles - *Eleanor Rigby*, Johnny Cash - *A Boy Named Sue*, The Police - *Don't Stand So Close To Me*, The Temptations - *Papa Was A Rollin' Stone*

Rihanna - *Umbrella,*

Jennifer Lopez - *Booty,*

Beyoncé Knowles - *Drunk In Love (feat. Jay-Z)*

Are these songs big storytellers? Do you stick around because you wanna know more about J-Lo's butt[1]? Does your life depend on finding out what Katy Perry has to say in verse 2? No. These songs - as 95% of all the songs on the radio today - describe moments, emotions, things. Story is dead. Or is it?

With this book I present to you an approach to songwriting that is all about telling a captivating story - without actually telling a story. In fact, each song named above does tell a story the addictive way and could have been written using the approach.

I'm not trying to reinvent the wheel here. Our goal is to write compelling, commercial tracks that fit into the radio format. But as you'll see, the Addiction Formula can help you get there much, much faster and with laser precision - over and over again. And best of all: It's so deviously simple you can learn it in 4 hours.

---

1 Ok, bad example.

IT'S REALLY YOURS.

On Making This Book Your B*tch

In order to get the most out of this book I highly recommend getting a highlighter, post-its and a pen. Highlight anything that is new to you or helps you in any way and mark the page with a labeled post-it.

If reading this book gives you an idea of any kind, whether related to what I have written or not, write it down immediately. These insights are often way more valuable than anything I could ever teach you. Highlighter, post-its, pen. Grab 'em now!

Secondly, I urge you to listen to at least half of the musical examples. Reading about a technique is not enough. You have to hear it in action. Too many songwriters have made the mistake to think that *understanding* something is just as good as knowing what it sounds like.

Do not be one of them.

I urge you to read this book next to a computer with youtube or spotify opened up and ready to go[1]. I put a lot of time and effort into finding examples that show different sides of the same technique, so listen to all of them even if you "get it" the first time.

Thirdly, if you haven't already, subscribe to my newsletter at holistic-songwriting.com. Every week, I share MASSIVE value, incl. some of my favorite techniques, like Trading Space and Base Pitches. Do it now!

And one more thing...

Before we get into how the Addiction Formula and Lyric-Less Storytelling works, make sure you read the overview on page 211 to get an idea of how the Formula fits into your writing process. You won't understand everything quite yet (and that's fine), but make sure you understand when to apply the formula to your songs.

---

1 If you're listening on youtube, note that some music videos have special intros different from the album version meaning that some of the times given in this book will be offset. In this case just try to find a lyric video - they often use the version from the album.

DISCLAIMER

We are primarily concerned with commercial music in this book. If this contradicts your artistic integrity, let me say a few words because I used to think very much like you.

If you want to make music that is completely free from conventions, pop music is not the place for you. Pop heavily relies on an element of recognition to help you relate quicker to a new song. Some songs are more obvious about it, using similar melodies, grooves or sounds as other hits while others are more sophisticated with it. That's just how it is. However, the pop rules that do exist still allow you to be immensely creative and original.

Think of the top 200 as a party that you can only go to if you dress up in a smoking. Does that change your personality or who you are? Of course not.

So what about artistic integrity? Too many times I have found this term to just mean "ego". If you are not willing to play by *any* rules, don't be surprised if you are not invited to the party.

But stay with me, I think once you learn what the rules are you will realize that they can be used with good intentions, i.e. musically. And we all agree that there should never be musical compromise in favor of commercialism.

PART 1:
ENERGY CURVES

In this part you will learn:

✓ What the Addiction Formula can do for your songs
✓ What a compelling energy curve looks like
✓ How to create your own energy curve from scratch

HOLISTIC SONGWRITING:
The Interdependency Problem

If you've ever tried to teach someone anything about songwriting you might have realized how hard it is to teach something if you have to keep all possibilities in mind. For example, if you tell your student that a chorus needs to be big, he might (correctly) argue that the chorus of Usher's *Climax* is in fact tiny.

The difficulty is that every element in a song is interdependent of its surroundings. Examining one element at a time is like studying an organ in the human body: take it out of its context and it will stop working.

And this marks the big problem with songwriting: There is so much stuff to keep in mind. A song needs to have great melody, harmony, rhythm, lyrics, production, arrangement, feeling, needs to be captivating, memorable and all of that in 3.5 minutes. Every single one of these elements is interdependent of one another. Change one and the rest has to follow suit.

This typically leads to a very inefficient writing process. Let's check it out, see if you recognize this from somewhere.

Friedemann Findeisen proudly presents:

10 OVERLY COMPLICATED STEPS TO WRITING A CONVOLUTED SONG

1) Start out with one element, let's say harmony.

2) Add a melody that goes with those chords.

3) Spend hours trying to find lyrics that fit both your melody and harmony.

4) Write parts for the other instruments that fit everything you have so far.

5) Write the next sections of the song in the exact same fashion.

6) Try to find musicians that go well with the song and record them.

7) Attempt to make all your different ideas in your song fit together through production.

8) Put song on soundcloud.

9) Be disappointed when no one listens to it.

10) Die alone and without anyone ever hearing your song (your cats don't count).

With this approach, there are two ways your music will end up sounding:

> Your song sounds like a random collection of different sections pasted together or
> it all sounds the same if you were too scared to deviate too far from your initial idea.

So your song will either weird out your audience or bore the crap out of them. These options aren't great and yet 99% of the songs I hear at conservatories and amongst to-be professionals suffer from this.

The next step for a songwriter is keeping a structure in mind when writing. You may know after you've written your first section that you've written a chorus and that you need to structure the rest of your song around it. That's a big step in the right direction - you're starting to see the forrest for the trees.

However, you're still moving from one element of your song to the next. You still start out with one element and adjust all the following elements to the previous ones. This can only lead to complications because all the following elements need to fit every single former element.

Most people know this problem from writing an entire song and then slapping on some lyrics. This rarely works out, because they need to work with so many existing elements now - the melody, the rhythm of the melody, the mood of the song, the structure, the arrangement, etc. I'm sure you have been in this situation before and you know it's a living hell.

Imagine working for Mercedes as a manufacturer and having to adjust to what everyone else is doing all the time. Sally from marketing comes in and tells you the motor needs to be bigger because it will sell better. 5 minutes later, Ron, the engineer, tells you it needs to be smaller to fit into the car. This obviously is a terrible way of running a company with everyone talking to everyone.

Yet this is how most songwriters write their songs. Every new element, be it lyrics, melody or instruments, needs to fit into whatever's already there, even if they are asking for entirely different things. Maybe you've written a fantastic melody but your lyrics just won't fit its rhythm. Or you have some great chord progressions but can't find the right arrangement for them. So what do you do? You compromise. You write a nonsensical line in favor of your melody or revert the chords to a standard power progression. Isn't that a shame.

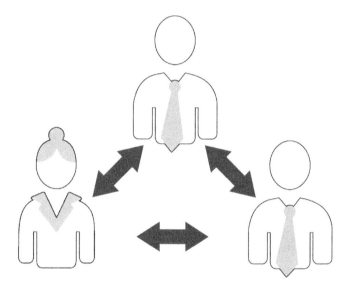

Let's get back to Mercedes. Maybe you've already figured out that what really would help this company is someone in charge, someone who makes the decisions for everyone. Someone with a vision and a plan.

This changes things. You now know exactly what it is you need to build - you just ask your boss. If two co-workers come over to tell you conflicting things, you let your boss settle the discussion for you. Done.

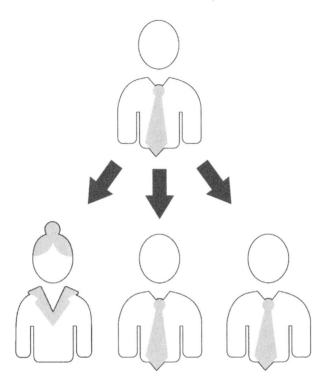

The same goes for songwriting. There needs to be a "boss", a governing principle that guides our writing process. This way, we don't need to cross-check everything new we write with what we already have, we just consult our "boss", our approach.

This book is about such an approach, which, again, is a governing principle you can use to write more coherent songs. It is *not* a technique or element. Instead, it *manages* all the elements of your song. This way, you're taking a holistic view of the whole writing process, where you understand how the different elements work together, instead of working on one element at a time.

Congratulations, you've just been promoted from mediator to manager. Now what would be a great governing principle for your songs? What is important no matter which genre or style you write in? That's what we will get to in the next chapter.

SUMMARY:

✓ This book will teach you a governing principle that guides all the other elements in your song.

HOW TO SOUND GEFÄHRLICH:
The Key To Captivating An Audience

When I was studying jazz guitar in Germany, I had a teacher called Florian Enderle. Imagine Matt Damon wearing a pair of Groucho Glasses: That's Florian.

Florian was and still is my favourite teacher because of his little anecdotes that he would share with us from time to time. One such an anecdote was about his guitar teacher who had taught him a very valuable lesson:

"You Got To Sound Gefährlich."

"Gefährlich" [pronounced *g'fair,lish*] is German for "dangerous", so the phrase translates to "you got to sound *dangerous*"[1].

This simple advice has completely changed the way I think about composition and it is a major component of the Addiction Formula.

---

1 Florian's teacher was American and had somehow picked up this word from him.

But what does it mean? It means you want your audience to feel endangered. You want to grab 'em by the throat with your music and create a compelling universe that pulls them in and is very hard to leave.

This is the key to good songwriting for me, and it is the ultimate goal of the Addiction Formula: Creating a fascinating and memorable experience with your songs that keeps your audience hooked from start to finish.

Of course, you want to do this in such a way that they don't notice it. No big swooshes or explosions necessary. In fact, even the sweetest little folk song about your neighbor's cacti can sound *gefährlich*.

This is because the Addiction Formula is merely acting in the background. It is only audible for the initiated, but it is there, managing all the different elements of the song. Once you are aware of it, you will start hearing it in virtually any hit song out there.

This is the power of this formula: It has an enormous impact on an audience while at the same time being so subtle that it's only noticeable to the initiated. So while anyone knows that a hit song needs a catchy hook and a special something-something that makes you wanna dance, the vast majority of listeners have no idea that there is another level of "attraction" in songwriting.

So how does it work? Well, what has enslaved you in the past? Maybe it was the TV series *Lost*, which you binge-watched in a week. Or you read a book and you just couldn't put it down. Maybe a video game or "funny cat" videos. Even if it's a more serious addiction like alcohol or drugs, what do all of these have in common? What makes them so enticing?

It's the principle of *gratification* & *anticipation*. You get something - a big revelation in Lost, a kiss in your book, a new area in your game, an especially funny cat video, a high from taking drugs - which gets you into it (gratification), and then you wait for it to happen again (anticipation). So you push through the boring episodes, read pages of long, boring descriptions in your book, keep dying over and over again during a difficult section in your game, spend hours clicking through unfunny cat videos and deal with withdrawal symptoms.

This seems like a terrible to-do list for a day and yet we do stuff like this all the time. The prospect of getting something is just too great to stop, even if the process is tedious.

Secondly, the most addictive things in the world have a way of forcing you into coming back: Movies, books and TV series use cliffhangers to create unbearable tension that can only be resolved by gratification. The longer you stay off of cigarettes, the more you will physically feel it. The only way to stop the feeling is to smoke. Gold diggers keep digging because in their mind their chances of finding gold go up the deeper they get.

This is all really fascinating stuff because the psychological principles that form the basis of all these addictions can also be used to make a listener addicted to your songs.

Imagine a song that subconsciously makes you want to listen. A song that hooks you, takes you to another place and keeps you there. A song you wanna play on repeat all day. This is the kind of song we want to write with this book. We are not so much interested in hooks, groove or lyrics but rather how to arrange them so they have the most impact.

So if we want to utilize this concept of anticipation and gratification for songwriting, there are three things we need to accomplish:

✓ Make the gratification parts increasingly satisfying to hook the audience and keep them coming back (these will typically be our choruses),

✓ Keep the periods of anticipation (or verses) interesting enough so we don't bore our audiences, and

✓ Find the perfect moments to switch between anticipation & gratification - if too much time passes, people will get bored and zone out; switch too quickly, and they will get confused.

Lucky for us, these points have been well-researched for over hundreds of years in the art of *storytelling*. A great story distributes its big moments well throughout its duration. Fact is: There is nothing more enticing than a good story.

Marketers - those people that *really* know how to get inside your head - use them all the time. Instead of telling you how great their product is, they start telling you a story[1].

Once you started, you can not go back. Be honest: Would you watch every single episode of *Breaking Bad* and then stop right before the last episode? Of course not. The Harry Potter book series wouldn't have been as successful as it was if people didn't want to know how the story continues[2]. It only makes sense to use the principles that make a great story work and use them to write more captivating songs.

Be aware that this is not just another book on writing more story-driven lyrics. Yes, we will get to that, but for the most part I want to talk about how you can tell a story just with your music. You can use this approach even if you only write instrumental tracks. This is why I refer to this idea as *Lyric-Less Storytelling*[3]. Our story then acts as a governing principle that is woven throughout

---

1 Godin, S. - *All Marketers Are Liars (Portfolio Trade, 2012)*

2 Which really means they want their moments of gratification: The first kiss, succeeding at school, triumphing over evil. The rest is merely anticipation.

3 Meaning it doesn't *need* lyrics to work.

every element of the song.

Note: Lyric-Less Storytelling is really only one of three factors that make a hit song (the others being *hook* and *groove*[1]). However, it is the most logical of the three and therefore the easiest to learn. And even more importantly: Learning this approach will give you a huge advantage in the business because *no one knows about it.*

Trust me on this one: *Everyone* knows about hook and groove. My *dentist* can tell you that. It doesn't take a lot to figure this out and it only takes a little luck to write a good hook or groove. I'm sure that you have already written a couple that could be a huge hit. The hard truth is that they are worthless if they're not presented right.

With this book I want to teach you how to place and introduce your hooks and grooves correctly so you get the most out of them and write songs that truly connect with people. So here is an overview about the things you are going to learn in the following pages of this book:

---

1 You can find programs on these and many other subjects at holistic-songwriting.com

First, we will look at how gratification and anticipation translate to music in order to really understand how we can practically force our audience to listen to us. We will go into great detail how to design an *energy curve* for your songs, which is a fantastic visual way of expressing the gratification/anticipation interplay. The question we will be asking in this part will be: "*What* is our story?"

In part 2 of this book, we will then go through each element of a song (such as arrangement, chords, production, etc.) and see how we can adapt them to our given energy curve. That means techniques, techniques, techniques. So we are concerned with *how* to tell our story.

And finally, in part 3, we will start with a chapter on creating your own techniques (and as far as I know, this is the only songwriting book *in the world* that does that!), followed by a 10-step guide to writing a song with the Addiction Formula. The question is: "How do we go from telling stories to becoming a storyteller?"

I am aware that you will probably want to skip over to part 2 immediately. Don't. This book follows a certain syntax which is designed to get you from where you are to mastery. In order to understand the techniques of part 2 properly, you first have to understand why and when to use them.

SUMMARY:

✓ Addiction has two components: *Gratification* (getting something that hooks you) and *Anticipation* (waiting for more Gratification).

✓ The Addiction Formula borrows heavily from storytelling to hook the listener and keep them invested. This happens on another level than merely singing about a story, which is why I refer to it as Lyric-Less Storytelling.

✓ Lyric-Less Storytelling is only one of the three pillars of a hit song. The other two are *Groove* and *Hook*.

ENERGY:

The Governing Principle

You may have heard the saying "music is universal". While I do not believe that to be true[1], there is one element all popular styles do seem to have in common. This element is *distribution of energy*.

Don't worry, I'm not gonna go all woo-woo on you and tell you that your couch should face your fireplace or that the stars need to align for you to write a hit song. What I mean is how the energy level of a song rises and falls.

The moments of highest energy (typically choruses) we already know as gratification. Moments of lower energy (verses) we know as anticipation.

As a professional songwriter, you have to be able to control energy with ease and precision. You have to know when to increase or decrease it and you know just how much and how to do it.

---

1 I remember my grandma calling Bryan Adams "just noise".

The easiest and most effective way to visualize energy is by using the energy curve model. This simple tool will help you tremendously when writing songs. For example, here is the energy curve for Clean Bandit's *Rather Be (feat. Jess Glynne):*

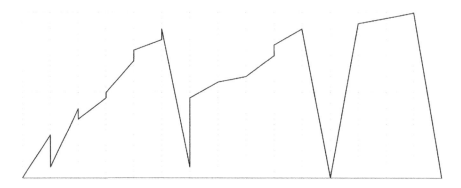

This curve shows you how the energy is distributed throughout the song. You can tell at a glance that the song is most intense during the last hook and that its lowest point of energy is during the intro and the primary bridge. So far, so good. Let's take a look at the elements it consists of.

Most people argue that energy is made up of *tension* and *release*. Unfortunately, these terms do not make much sense to me anymore in this day and age. While they might help analyzing Stravinsky, they seem a little unfitting to describe everything that is going on in a song of the 21st century. So let's fine-tune the terms to reflect a more modern approach to songwriting:

„Tension" is fine and we will use the term in this book, although I have a couple of adjustments to make to the definition which we will get to.

The word „Release" is problematic: It implies letting your audience drift away in their thoughts. This is not the goal of the Addiction Formula, where we want to keep the listener closely connected to the song.

Instead, I suggest using the words „tension" & „*hype*".

„Hype" describes a *relative energy level*. It can only be altered abruptly, not gradually: It usually jolts up or down every four or eight bars. Typically, it's the highest in the chorus and the lowest in the intro. If your song was a car, hype would be your gears.

And this is what hype looks like in an energy curve:

The elements that have the biggest influence on hype are:

✓ Arrangement (e.g. more instruments equals higher hype)

✓ Part-Writing (e.g. an instrument played loud is higher in hype)

✓ Rhythm (e.g. sections with few notes are low in hype)

USING TENSION

If there was no tension, hype and energy would be the same thing. However, when we are in a part of the song with low hype, we still want our audience to know that this is only temporary and that we will get bigger soon.

By increasing tension we let them know that we are approaching a moment of gratification. Tension is always gradual. If hype was your gears, this would be your gas pedal.

Here is what tension looks like in an energy curve:

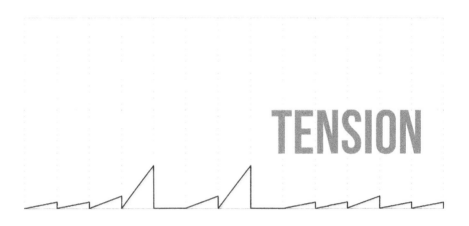

The elements that have the biggest influence on tension are:

✓ Harmony (e.g. ending on a V-chord)
✓ Part-Writing (e.g. slowly opening up a hi hat)
✓ Rhythm (e.g. increasing the number of notes played)
✓ Production (e.g. slowly opening up a filter)

To get the finished energy curve, simply add tension to hype. This will create a curve as shown here:

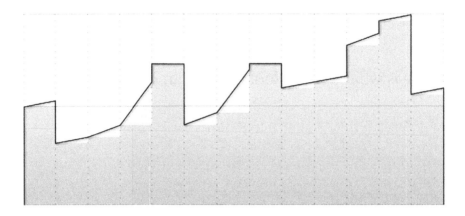

Note: There is a third, more complex element that determines your energy curve which we will get to in part II of this book. For now, I want you to focus on hype and tension. Make sure you really understand these before you read on, as we will get back to them time and time again in this book.

In future chapters, we won't be coloring in the hype levels anymore. This will force you to learn to see it in your mind when you look at an energy curve. I want you to get to a point where you can tell what is going on in a section at a quick glance.

So in other words, when you see this energy curve:

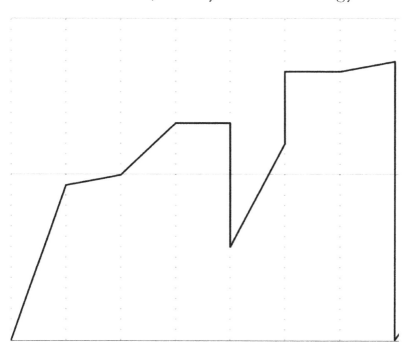

I want you to see this in your mind instead:

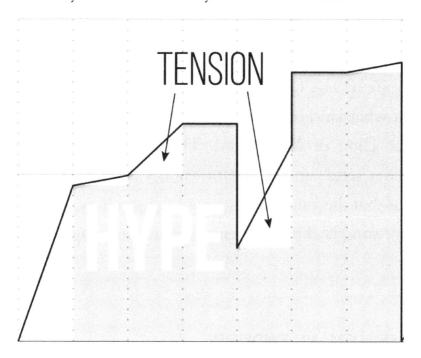

And there you have it: Your governing principle, your boss. This curve will control all the elements of your song. The quality of arrangement, harmony, rhythm, part-writing, lyrics and production all depend on getting this curve just right.

If your audience could draw your energy curve just from listening to your track you've done a good job. If the energy curve is an effective one to begin with (i.e. it follows the rules of addiction), you might even have a hit on your hands. In the next chapter, we will talk about how to create your own energy curve so you can start experimenting.

A QUICK NOTE ON LEVELS.

All the values described above - energy, hype and tension - are *relative*. Looking at them will give you no clue about what kind of song you are hearing - it could be Celine Dion or Motörhead. The graphs are drawn to fit the song's most extreme energy levels. This also means that the values also can not tell you how dynamic your song is: The difference between minimum and maximum energy can range from barely noticeable[1] to dramatic[2].

SUMMARY:

✓ Energy is made up of Tension and Hype.

✓ Hype is static and changes abruptly with each section of a song.

✓ Tension is dynamic and changes gradually. It is used to smooth out the blocky hype curve.

---

1 Robin Thicke - *Blurred Lines (feat. T.I. & Pharrell)*

2 Miley Cyrus - *Wrecking Ball*

THE PERFECT ENERGY CURVE
Let's Go For A Ride

In this chapter, we will talk about how you can design your own energy curve. I will give you the do's & don'ts and a step by step guide to creating your curve.

STEP 1: ENERGY PEAKS.

First, decide for a number of energy peaks. 3 is always a good start. It has its roots in the 3 movements of the sonata form and is by far the most popular. 2 or 4 is also possible. Note: These numbers don't count repetitions, so if the last chorus is repeated, it doesn't change the fact that it is still ONE energy peak.

STEP 2: PLACEMENT.

Next, you have to decide where to put the energy peaks and troughs. What it really comes down to is balancing repetition and change:

REPEAT	←	→	BALANCE	←	→	CHANGE
BORING	MEMORABLE BORING		MEMORABLE INTERESTING		INTERESTING CONVOLUTED	CONVOLUTED

Here are some examples: If you have 3 energy peaks, you could go for Chorus - Verse - Chorus - Verse - Chorus (not counting intros, pre-choruses, interludes, etc)[1] or the much more typical Verse - Chorus - Verse - Chorus - Prim. Bridge - Chorus[2]. 2 energy peaks, go for Verse - Chorus - Verse - Chorus[3]. With 4 choruses, you might want to start out your song with a chorus[4] or you simply add another bridge: Verse - Chorus - Verse - Chorus - Prim. Bridge - Chorus - Prim. Bridge - Chorus[5].

If you want to build a curve from scratch, here are 3 tips to help you get creative:

1) *End big.* You probably want a nice climax at the end of your song, so putting a chorus there is usually a good decision. However, ending on a bridge-like section can also be very effective if you want to suggest an open

---

1 Linkin Park - *Crawling*

2 Clean Bandit - *Rather Be (feat. Jesse Glynne)*, Sam Smith - *Stay With Me*

3 Mr. Probz - *Waves*

4 Pink - *Get This Party Started*, Eminem - *The Monster*, Iggy Azalea - *Change Your Life (feat. T.I.)*

5 Pharrell Williams - *Happy*

ending[1]. This is a pretty mean way of ending a song, because you're not giving your audience the gratification they want, but it also just might be the reason that they hit that replay button.

2) *Up, Up, Up.* One of the biggest problems I see many songwriters struggle with is writing a good second verse. This is due to the fact that many writers forget the simple fact that anything too predictable is boring. Think back to your latest addiction - for me it was watching Bob Ross' *Joy of Painting.* I was really into it when I started. I learned a lot. I had a great time and couldn't get enough of it. But after a while I kept seeing the same techniques over and over again and my excitement faded. Each episode felt the same.

This is equally true in music: *Repeat and you will lose your audience.* Make sure you give your song direction by changing small things here and there, preferably getting bigger as the song progresses. This is especially important when writing the second verse. Make sure you don't just repeat verse 1. This is one of the most com-

1 Justin Timberlake - *What Goes Around,* Seether - *Eyes Of The Devil,* Deftones - *Passenger (feat. Maynard James Keenan)*

mon mistakes songwriters make. You got your high-lighter, here's something to highlight:

> Bad technique (Same hype level as first verse):
> *"…And we're back to this again."*
> Good technique (Higher hype level than first verse):
> *"But wait, there's more!"*
> Great technique (Higher hype level & tension):
> *"Aaaaaand-"*

So make sure that the overall energy level throughout your song keeps going up (the only exception to this is using *Implied Tension*, which we will cover later). The most gratifying songs are those that put their biggest moment at the end, with the rest of the song building up to it.

3) *The Golden Mean or: The 1-2-3 Rule.* Following this ratio when structuring your song usually leads to pleasing results. Some christians see this number (a little less than 2/3) as proof of an intelligent designer, which has also led to the name *Divine Proportion*.

And indeed, there are countless examples to be found

in nature for this ratio, such as the human heart beat, the amount of petals on pine cones, flower petals, seed heads, even the human face, DNA molecules and spiral galaxies.

Whether woo-woo or not, the ratio has found its way into aesthetics. The Pantheon in Rome is designed following the proportion, just like the Mona Lisa, the statue of David, the logos for Apple, Toyota, Pepsi, etc. The golden mean has become a representative for beauty.

We can find the ratio in music as well. For example, the form of Debussy's *La Mer* corresponds exactly to the golden mean, as do most of the works by Béla Bartók. There is much discussion about this phenomenon as there is no evidence that any of the composers consciously sought out to use the ratio in their compositions, but whether they did or not, the ratio is there.

I don't expect you to believe this whole divine proportion story (although it is a fascinating topic, don't you think?), so here is a more psychological way of thinking about it:

Have you ever heard about the "rule of three"? It says that *all good things come in threes*. By repeating something you create the expectation of a pattern. The audience is conditioned to believe that they will hear the same thing over and over again.

But instead, you surprise them with a completely new situation. It's exactly the same kind of principle that makes all those jokes work:

A Priest and a Rabbi walk into a bar; the Minister ducked.

You pretend to set up a pattern and then break with it.

So let's look at today's songwriting and see how the golden mean is represented in standard song form:

As you can see, there seems to be an unwritten rule about how many times you can repeat a section before something new has to happen. For you this just means that if you're making up your own energy curve, build in this 1-2-3 rule as much as you can as it strikes a perfect balance between repetition and change[1]:

STEP 3: SMOOTH OUT THE BUILD-UPS.

This is the step that most people are not aware of but it is absolutely crucial for writing a great song. It has to do with anticipation: If we are not looking forward to the chorus musically, then why would our audience? So for this, we will zoom in a little on our energy curve and just look at one build up from an energy trough to a peak:

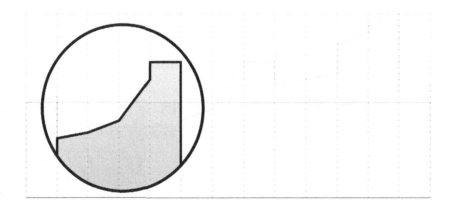

---

1 You might also know it from blues form.

This step is about slowly building up the energy to the next chorus. Note this common mistake: It doesn't matter if you write something *different*, if your energy levels don't change, your audience will get bored very quickly.

There are three ways to increase anticipation:
➤ By increasing the hype levels every 4 or 8 bars,
➤ By using tension or
➤ By combining the two.
Let's see what this looks like:

1) INCREASE OF HYPE LEVELS[1]

This is the most basic way of creating anticipation.

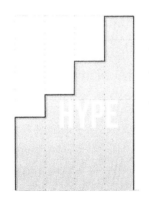

Since the energy is going up and up and up, we get a feeling of direction towards the next energy peak rather than remaining where we are. Using only hype to create anticipation can sound a little jumpy because there's nothing that leads into the following 4 or 8 bars so it isn't widely used. However, in the right

1 Serj Tankian - *The Unthinking Majority (notice the abrupt jumps in hype every 4 bars from 0:32 onwards).*

context, it can be used creatively to create a chaotic or surprising effect.

2) USING TENSION[1]

A much smoother way of leading up to an energy peak

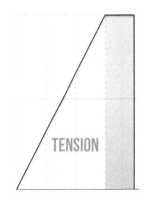

is using tension. This is the inferior method of reaching a peak because it has more direction than just using hype levels. This technique makes your energy peak stand out much more by introducing a certain aura of mystery that the others don't have. However, in the real world there are not a lot of songs using only tension to reach an energy peak.

So it is possible to use hype and tension individually. However, it is much more common to combine the two, which we will look at next.

---

1 Katy Perry - *Firework (build-up at 0:39 - 1:10). There is a slight increase of hype at 0:55, but most of the energy curve is determined by tension.*

3) COMBINING HYPE & TENSION[1]

This is the most commonly used type of raising the

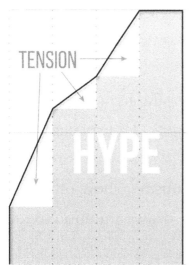

energy level over a period of multiple sections. It has a great sense of direction, is straight-forward and connects with your audience big time. Knowing how to control both hype and tension therefore is key to writing commercially successful songs.

STEP 4: SMOOTH OUT THE TRANSITIONS.

Now that we've looked at an entire build-up, let's zoom in even more and look at how the energy level can change from one section to the next.

1 Sia - *Chandelier (build-up at 1:40 - 2:03)*

Want to practice your newly-learned skills? See if you can guess the definitions just from looking at the pictures. If you can't, go back and review hype & tension.

1) JUMP[1]

Definition: Increasing hype step-wise.

Best Case Scenario: Unexpected, in-your-face.

Worst Case Scenario: Chaotic, confusing, show-offy, irritating ("Shhhh, the neighbors!"), draws attention to the arrangement.

Notes: This is a move that is often seen when going from verse to verse cont. or from prim. bridge to prim. bridge cont. It's the easiest of all transitions to use and when used subtly it is a great addition to your set of tools.

2) SMOOTH[2]

Definition: Using hype & tension to increase energy.

Best Case Scenario: Exciting, anticipating, beautiful, compelling, interesting.

Worst Case Scenario: Predictable.

---

1 The Black Eyed Peas - *I Gotta Feeling (jumping transition at 1:00)*
2 Adele - *Set Fire To The Rain (build-up 0:55 to 1:00)*

Notes: This is the most popular transition in hit songs. It has a great sense of direction and works in almost every situation.

3) DROP[1]

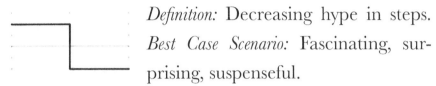

Definition: Decreasing hype in steps.
Best Case Scenario: Fascinating, surprising, suspenseful.

Worst Case Scenario: Disappointing, confusing, boring.

Notes: This is the typical transition from chorus back to verse. Making this move work can be tricky, because you can easily lose some listeners with it. Using tension or implied tension (which we will get to in part 2) right after a drop will usually save your ass.

4) SURPRISE[2]

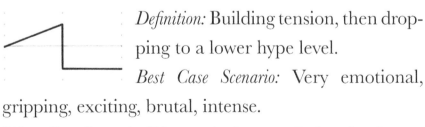

Definition: Building tension, then dropping to a lower hype level.
Best Case Scenario: Very emotional, gripping, exciting, brutal, intense.

Worst Case Scenario: Disappointing, confusing, boring.

---

1 Rihanna - *Disturbia (transition at 1:19)*

2 Usher - *Climax (transition at 1:14)*, Katy Perry - *Dark Horse (feat. Juicy J., transition at 1:17)*

Notes: This is more of an effect, which can be very useful when transitioning from chorus to verse or prim. bridge. It feels like you are sucking the air out of the room. Note that you're running into the same problems as with a regular Drop.

5) OVERSHOOT[1]

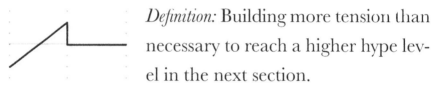

Definition: Building more tension than necessary to reach a higher hype level in the next section.

Best Case Scenario: Implying underlying turmoil

Worst Case Scenario: Disappointing, confusing, boring.

Notes: Don't ever use it. Pretending to go somewhere and then not doing it is effectively telling your listener that they've waited all this time for nothing.

6) FALSE PROMISE[2]

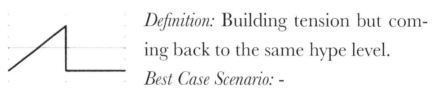

Definition: Building tension but coming back to the same hype level.

Best Case Scenario: -

Worst Case Scenario: Very disappointing, boring, confus-

---

1 Mark Ronson - *Uptown Funk (feat. Bruno Mars, transition at 1:06)*

2 Usher - *Climax (transition at 1:14)*, Refused - *New Noise (transition at 0:47)*

ing, draws attention to the arrangement.

Notes: Even more dangerous than overshooting. Use at extreme caution or you will burn yourself! Always follow by using implied tension. And don't wait too long with your moment of gratification or you will piss off your audience.

7) FLATLINE[1]

Definition: Keeping the hype level unchanged.

Best Case Scenario: -

Worst Case Scenario: Your audience dies of boredom (or turns off your song).

Notes: This is also a tricky one. If you have something really special that will keep your audience listening one way or another (such as implied tension, a fantastic vocal performance or an especially groovy drum beat), this might work, but there still is no reason *not* to go up (unless you have a ballad and don't want it to be too busy). When in doubt, always go up.

---

1 Taylor Swift - *Shake It Off (transition at 0:17)*, Katy Perry - *Hot N Cold (transition at 0:18)*. Note that both of these happen in the middle of the first verse.

8) LIFT[1]

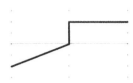

Definition: Building less tension than necessary to transition to a higher hype level

Best Case Scenario: Great direction, moving, huge.

Worst Case Scenario: Chaotic, confusing, show-offy, irritating, draws attention to the arrangement.

Notes: If you like writing big, impressive choruses, then from now on this is your go-to move for transitioning into them. It packs more of a punch than a smooth transition, clearly establishes the chorus and has great direction.

9) NEGATIVE TENSION[2]

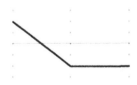

Definition: Gradually decreasing the energy to reach a lower hype level.

Best Case Scenario: Smooth, beautiful

Worst Case Scenario: Confusion, disorientation.

Notes: I'm listing this transition merely for completion's sake here as it isn't widely used. Negative tension can be achieved by using downlifters, certain kinds of drum

---

1 Miley Cyrus - *Wrecking Ball (transition at 0:41)*

2 Taylor Swift - *We Are Never Ever Getting Back Together (transition at 1:05)*

fills or stripping out instruments in the middle of a section.

So there you have them, 9 ways to transition from one section to another. Make sure you know all of them and when to use them.

Note: It is possible to add tension exclusively to the last couple of beats of a section, for example by having the drummer play a short fill. This still adds tension to the whole section, the overall tension is just much lower. So the correct way of drawing this would be:

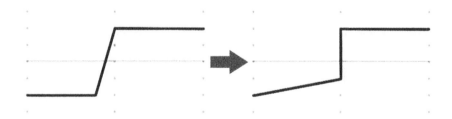

(S)HIT TEST #1: THE FRIEND TEST

One of the best ways of learning to write with the Addiction Formula is giving your song to a friend of yours and asking them to draw an energy curve for your song (you should briefly explain hype and tension). Then analyze their curve - is it what you expected?

Let's do it together to show you what I mean. The following curve is derived from a song a colleague of mine wrote recently:

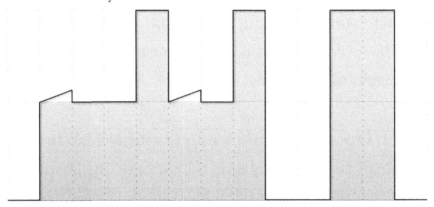

Take a minute to find all the good and bad about this curve for yourself before you read on. What works, what could be better?

Let's start with the things my buddy did right:

✓ He does have 3 evenly-spaced energy peaks,
✓ The lowest point of energy is in the first introduction,
✓ The prim. bridge brings in change.

So what could be better?

➤ The overall energy is not going up. He needs to either make his first verse smaller or the second verse bigger. The same goes for the choruses.

- There is no build-up to the big moments. The verses and bridge should systematically increase their hype levels and use tension to smooth out the hard edges.
- Non-sensical build-ups. The verses build up to nothing - you can see this by the energy going up and dropping back down again. We know this as a False Promise. Very dangerous.

Make sense? Go do it with your songs.

QUESTION:

Are there hit songs out there *not* using the Addiction Formula?

ANSWER: There are no pop hits that I'm aware of that don't use it at all. It really seems to be used all over the board - a real "rule of hit writing" you could say. However, every now and then you'll have a song that stretches the rules, 3 of which I want to show you now:

Mark Ronson - *Uptown Funk ft. Bruno Mars:* While largely following the Addiction Formula, the 1st and 2nd verse have identical energy levels, which makes the beginning of the 2nd verse an opportunity to turn this song off (we will discuss this on page 207).

The Black Eyed Peas - *I Gotta Feeling:* Although this song does use tension & hype very effectively for the most part, the second verse is lower in energy than the first and the second and third chorus are very far apart. Hype changes every 16 bars (instead of every 8 bars).

Beyoncé - *Run the World (Girls), 7/11:* The way the attention of the listener is guided through these songs is phenomenal, albeit unusual. They don't follow the 1-2-3 rule and chorus and verse don't stand out as clear energy peaks or troughs. While both songs follow the Addiction Formula, they use it in a very original way, so make sure you give these songs a listen.

SUMMARY:

The 4 steps to designing your energy curve are:

✓ Determine the amount of your big moments. 3 is always a good start.

✓ Placement. End big, globally increase tension, 1-2-3 rule (1 introduce - 2 repeat - 3 change)

✓ Smooth out the build-ups. Use hype, tension or a combination of the two to accomplish this.

✓ Smooth out the transitions. The possibilities are jump, smooth, drop, surprise, overshoot, false promise, flatline, lift and negative tension.

Now I know you're probably itching to find out how to set energy levels in your song, but before we get to that I want to share one more thing with you: The most popular energy curve in the world…

HOLLYWOOD'S SECRET FORMULA

The Most Popular Form In The World

In this chapter, I want to introduce you to the most popular and effective energy curve there is in songwriting. There are many more curves that work, but I always keep this *"Hollywood curve"* in the back of my mind when I'm writing - even when I'm using a different curve. I am almost a hundred percent sure that you've used this curve before, but I want to show you why it works so well and point out a couple of things you can do to make it even more powerful so it drills down right into your audience's mind.

Screenwriters have perfected the art of storytelling over decades. They know exactly how to unravel a mystery, when to be funny and when to be dramatic, how to make us fall in love with the main characters and how to make us hate the bad guy.

In his book *Screenplay* (1979), Syd Field introduced the

world's now most popular structure to film[1]. Nearly every movie you know follows this structure. It consists of three basic acts:

1) *Setup*, where we are introduced to the hero and his problem (sometimes called the *inciting incident*).
2) *Confrontation*, where the shit hits the fan. Our hero's attempts to bring the adventure to a halt only result in more complications.
3) *Resolution*, where the hero has to face his ultimate obstacle, and in doing so either succeeds or fails.

Whether we are talking about the *Lion King*, *The Matrix* or *Insidious*, this structure is always present. You have probably seen hundreds of movies that used this structure, but never noticed it. Hollywood swears by it. Scripts that don't follow the formula get turned down. But why is it so effective? Says Daniel McInerny[2]:

1 He based it on the dramatic structure by Gustav Freytag which in turn is based on Aristoteles' 2-act structure that had an act before and after tragedy strikes (notice that the midpoint still plays a major part in Aristoteles' 2-act structure). In *Poetics*, Aristotle also talks about a 12-act (!) structure. We will come across this number a couple of times, too.

2 "On that Good 'Ole Hollywood Ending", Aleteia, Nov 29, 2013

"The central reason why three-act structure resonates so profoundly with the human spirit, such that we never tire of its rhythms, is that it allows us, in a most compressed and evident way, to contemplate our lives in miniature. Three-act structure is the structure of life. It is the imitation of ourselves being thrown into an adventure not of our choosing, and of working out a resolution to it in which we ultimately either succeed or fail.[1]"

Let's take a close look at what the 3-act structure has in common with music. To illustrate my point and to make this whole shebang a little more entertaining, I wrote you a little script following our structure. Your job is to find commonalities between this story and standard song structure. Ready? Let's go.

ACT 1

We get to meet John, our hero. John is a family man in a mid-life crisis. He is bitter and also a bit of a wimp. He lives his life not knowing that within a day, everything will be different.

---

1 Just an interesting observation here: Did you notice Daniel's choice of words in his article? "Resonate", "Rhythms"…

The first couple of minutes have to win people over or they will leave the theater. This *opening* sets the mood for the rest of the film and introduces our characters. It marks the lowest energy level in the entire movie.

When John hears that he is being drafted, a world ends for him. He does not want to go. He has to say goodbye to all his loved ones.

Just as we begin to like our character and want him to be happy, they are confronted with a problem. Something rattles their status quo.

ACT 2

John arrives in the middle of a raging war. He is confronted with death and misery.

Act 2 typically occurs at the 30-minute mark (after a fourth of the film). This is where we fully realise the weight of our problem for the first time. It is the second moment after the introduction that can make or break a film, as it sets the *highest* level of energy. Combined with the introduction this gives the audience an idea of the dynamic range of the movie that they are seeing.

After standing out as the worst soldier in his unit, John realises he has to toughen up if he wants to make it out alive. He trains hard and what do you know - becomes the first in his unit to learn how to assemble his gun in under a minute. When a fellow soldier gets into serious trouble during an exercise, John is the only one brave enough to help him, which earns him the respect of his fellow soldiers and what used to be a unit becomes friends.

Things slowly sink in. The character tries to deal with the problem. He slowly gets used to his new situation and becomes a different person. He has to, because trouble is lurking around the corner.

THE MIDPOINT

The big battle comes and John's unit fights hard - and emerges triumphantly. John is skyping with his family who is relieved that everything is ok, when suddenly a group of people enter his tent and kidnap John, killing one of his friends. Cut off from his unit, John is on his own.

The exact middle of the movie (*60-minute mark or 60-page mark*) is where our second big moment happens. It comes in strong, and we naturally assume it will be the big finale, but something unexpected happens: We move into new terrain.

ACT 3

John is kept prisoner for a long time, grows a beard and loses a lot of weight. After half a year of Imprisonment he finally sees a chance to escape. He manages to run for about an hour before they find him. When everything seems lost and John is to be executed on the spot, suddenly bullets start flying and one of his evildoers falls to the ground dead. It's his unit that's come back for him. Together, they overrun their enemies. John returns as a war hero.

When everything seems as though we couldn't possibly go back to normality our second turning point happens and things very quickly move toward the climax.

John takes a flight back home. When he sees his family, he's too tired to smile. He is not the man he used to be.

The ending can be a big finale or it can end on a smaller, more personal note. It returns to the status quo of the introduction, but since a lot of things have happened in the course of our story, things are slightly different. This is where our character development really becomes obvious.

Study the curve on the opposing page. See how well that translates to songs? See how the energy moves up and down similarly, how the arrangement reflects the story? Do you see the energy curve, the 1-2-3 rule, the way tension and hype interact in this story?

So what can we learn from this Hollywood formula? Well, it basically gives us a great energy curve to work with.

Its properties are:
✓ There are 3 pretty much evenly-spaced energy peaks,
✓ The peaks are preceded by troths that build up to the peaks,
✓ The biggest energy peak is last,
✓ The lowest point of energy is in the first act,
✓ After the second energy peak, the energy goes way down.

THE 3-ACT STRUCTURE

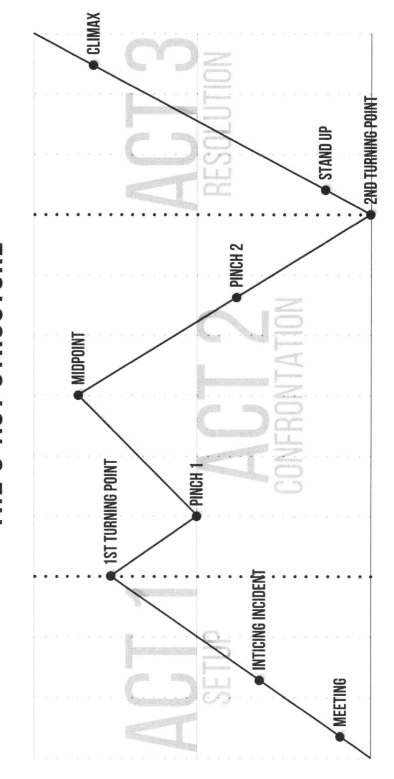

You can probably already tell that we're talking about the following form:

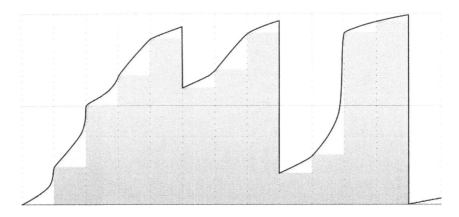

(Intro, Verse, Verse cont. Pre-Chorus, Chorus, Verse, Pre-Chorus, Chorus, Bridge, Bridge cont., Chorus, Chorus, Outro)

The closer you are to this structure, the more your song will take advantage of its benefits.

Have you ever had the pleasure of falling asleep during a movie? Then you know that if a movie does not deliver enough big moments of gratification, you are likely to zone out sooner or later.

If we (subconsciously) feel like a section in a song is going on for too long, we get restless. The need for change is so great that we create it ourselves by changing the station.

Screenwriters call this *pacing*. For example, as a writer for action films or thrillers, you are expected to have a big moment every ten pages (which equals roughly every ten minutes). Otherwise your movie will drag. Luckily, this principle is already built into the hollywood form.

Let's go literal here for a second and assume a standart movie is 120 minutes. If we need a moment every 10 minutes, that gives us 12 moments for the whole movie.

Well, how many moments does a song have (assuming that one section is 8 bars and not counting the beginning of the song of course)?

1. Beginning Verse
2. Verse Continued
3. Beginning Pre-Chorus
4. Beginning Chorus
5. Beginning Second Verse
6. Beginning Second Pre-Chorus

7. Beginning Second Chorus
8. Beginning Prim. Bridge
9. Prim. Bridge Continued
10. Beginning Third Chorus
11. Beginning Fourth Chorus
12. Beginning Outro

12 exactly. And if that wasn't weird enough already, now notice that the beginning of the second chorus (midpoint) is at *exactly* half.

Weird, isn't it? How mankind subconsciously produces things following the same principles over and over again? From my own experience, I could show you similar structures in marketing, card magic and public speaking. Like the golden ratio, there seems to be something about this structure that resonates with people, almost like a key that fits perfectly into the part of our brain that holds our attention.

SUMMARY:

✓ The most popular energy curve in pop music by far is the "Hollywood Curve"

✓ A song written with the Hollywood Formula is structured as follows: Intro, verse, verse cont., pre-chorus, chorus, verse, pre-chorus, chorus, prim. bridge, prim. bridge cont., chorus, chorus, outro.

Now let's zoom in a little bit more and go from the whole movie to its scenes in the next chapter. So we're now slowly transitioning from theory to practical songwriting.

AND... SCENE!

Let's Write A Thriller

Let's look at each section of the hollywood structure from a dramatic standpoint and see how we can keep them interesting.

If you want to be a master songwriter, the one thing you have to completely internalize is understanding the different sections of your song. I will showcase how the hollywood structure works here and leave it up to you to apply what you learn to your own structures.

THE INTRO.

The intro really holds a special place in dramaturgy, as it presents the status quo. We get to see our hero before he is thrown into all that drama, we get to experience him in his day-to-day life.

The screenwriter's job here is to make sure that our hero seems like someone we would like to be friends with. If the writer fails to do this, we will simply not care enough to see what happens to him next.

In music, this is equally true: With the intro, we set our status quo, show the listener what our song looks like at its lowest energy level. This is why it's much harder to write songs that start strong - where do you go from there?

Sound is very important during these first few seconds of our song. It's like our hero: we either like him or we do not. So make sure your instruments sound great from the get go.

THE FIRST VERSE.

Our now beloved best friend has a problem. A series of events is set in motion that will lead to a big bang very soon. The hero tries to get out of his situation but only winds up deeper in the rabbit hole.

The lyrics introduce what our song is about. The singer's tone of voice shows us how he feels. We see he has something he needs to get off his chest. He's vaguely describing his situation, our anticipation rises. We want to know what's going on, want to know what the fuss is all about.

Just like in the movies, the verse is there to introduce us to the problem and at the same time foreshadow the chorus.

The biggest mistake you can make in the verse (really in arranging in general) is to write without looking at the big picture. Look at the 3 act graph again. The first act is not a horizontal line! Instead, see the verse as a springboard into the chorus. It is a period of anticipation, there to increase the excitement until the big bang! So build hype and add tension.

THE FIRST PRE-CHORUS.

The pre-chorus is, as the name already suggests, not a self-contained section. It is just a *Transitional Bridge*. See it as a kind of modulation from the verse to the chorus. Even more so than the verse it only has one job to do: Creating tension. If there is ever a section in which you can get out all your techniques for creating tension, this is it. So an electronic producer might introduce an *Uplifter* or *Noise Sweep* here (increase in tension). Similarly, the melody typically goes higher (increase in hype) and therefore forms a pivot point between a low verse and a high chorus.

THE FIRST CHORUS.

The first turning point in film displays the scope of the movie to the audience: If it is too small, we will expect the rest of the movie to be small. On the other hand, we do not want to oversell it either, as we want people to feel satisfied about our ending as well. It is a difficult balance act of figuring out just how big your first chorus should be.

I have found the following to work well: Write your last chorus first. Make it as big as possible and copy/paste it to create your first chorus. Now strip out everything that isn't strictly needed to convey the feeling of gratification. Maybe your percussion can go or a pad. Maybe the backing vocals can go. Never delete for this kind of thing, always mute. You will want to try out different combinations.

Make sure you always listen in context: There needs to be a noticeable jump in hype from pre-chorus to chorus. If it's not strong enough, either thin out the pre-chorus (this in turn might mean thinning out the verse as well) or add back elements to the chorus.

THE INTERLUDE.

Like the pre-chorus, the interlude (or *post-chorus*) is another type of transitional bridge that can be used to transition from a high-energy chorus to a less energetic second verse.

However, unlike the pre-chorus, it typically does have its own purpose. It is almost always instrumental and focused on groove. Although mostly used in rock music as a means of reintroducing the main riff[1], it is also often used in pop music. Here, it often takes the role of a dance part[2] or introduces the hook[3].

THE SECOND VERSE.

After the first big moment hit us, we realize we are in big, big trouble. Now what do we wanna see? Do you want to see the hero to go back to his everyday life and pretend that nothing has happened? Or do you want to see them deal with their problem? This is called *character development* in writing - we want our hero to go through

---

1 Staind - *Fill Me Up*

2 Katy Perry - *Dark Horse*

3 Rihanna - *Umbrella (feat. Jay-Z, depending on the version at 0:50 or 1:18)*, Clean Bandit - *Rather Be (feat. Jess Glynne, 1:20)*

some changes. No one goes through a big bang without rethinking their life, so returning to "problem" level feels almost inhumane.

While the first chorus is the hardest to write, the second verse is the hardest to arrange. Too many writers lose all their pep here and go back to the energy level of their first verse[1]. Remember: You want to be moving forward! Find a way to make your second verse bigger than your first while keeping it in anticipation mode. *Implied Tension* is an excellent way of doing this, as we will discuss when we talk about arrangement.

THE SECOND PRE-CHORUS.

The same goes as for the first pre-chorus: Just make sure you build to the second chorus. After the more intense second verse the second pre-chorus is also more energetic than the first. However, its role as a pivot point has not changed.

THE SECOND CHORUS.

When the shit hits the fan for a second time in our

---

1 As we saw in *Uptown Funk*.

movie, make sure you are not just rehashing the first chorus. Drama needs to keep going *up*! Find a subtle way to make your second chorus slightly bigger than the first (unmute one or two new tracks or use any other technique from part 2 of this book).

THE PRIMARY BRIDGE (AKA BRIDGE OR C-PART).

Imagine you are the person who invented the 3 act scheme. If you want your finale to have the proper bang, what can you do after the second chorus to make that bang even more impactful?

Your frist thought would be to go smaller. Problem is, you can't return to your status quo - your hero has been through too much! Just going back to another verse feels anticlimactic and predictable. So what do you do? You go into unexplored terrain, you completely change the game. This is the moment where Jenko & Schmidt from *22 Jump Street* turn against each other. When the villagers in *Beauty and the Beast* start their hunt for the Beast. It's the moment that completely changes the game. Nothing will ever be the same, the status quo seems destroyed.

Honestly, you can't go wrong here in terms of ideas. Anything is possible and people will be ok with it. It is a good moment to bring in new sounds (such as solo instruments or a rap), change keys, go crazy. Prim. bridges are a great moment for creativity. Do not slag them off as not important though! The prim. bridge *does* have a purpose! It is there to provide contrast, to show a different side of the problem, to surprise. It is up to you whether you want to go small or big, just make sure you introduce enough tension to drive your song towards your last chorus.

THE THIRD AND FOURTH CHORUS OR FINALE.

This is it - the moment everybody's been waiting for. The big shootout, the wedding, the tragic death, the realization that christmas miracles do happen[1]. A movie's finale needs to be huge and satisfying so people leave the theater telling everyone what a great time they had.

The third chorus is completely dependent on what happens in chorus #4, so we will look at that one first. The fourth chorus or finale is not as set in stone as the

---

1 Usually in separate films, though.

rest of the song. Whereas before everything needed to be organised, at this point we have already heard the chorus three times and can allow ourselves to go a little crazy.

Your party is nearing its end - the men wear their ties around their heads and the women start taking off their shoes. This part is really for everyone who loved the party and who wants the night to end on a high point.

No reason to be shy here, because everyone who wasn't into it from the start has left already anyways. If people wouldn't want you to go crazy at this point they too would have already left.

Don't fall into the trap of just repeating your chorus two more times here. There *needs* to be some kind of build up in the last chorus, however subtle.

Here are a couple of examples that work well here, and we will cover many more in part 2:

Add new instruments. Guitar solos, Strings, Horn parts, Synths, backing vocals all work well[1].

Change the melody slightly so it hits more top notes. This really builds up some energy and puts your last chorus in the highest overall range[2].

Let the background vocals take over the main melody (panned all the way to the sides) and your main singer improvises over it[3]. You are creating your energy by effectively just adding another layer on top of your chorus *and* by really opening up your stereo panorama. This is a great technique because it gives your audience the chance to sing along with the background choir if they just want to sing the chorus.

Change the lyrics. This approach is overlooked by many, but it works very well. Introducing new lyrics to your

---

1 Sam Smith - *Stay With Me*, Linkin Park - *Numb*, Alien Ant Farm - *Smooth Criminal*
2 Pharrell Williams - *Happy*, Sam Smith - *Stay With Me*, Staind - *Fill Me Up*
3 Aliyah - *Try Again*, Jessie J - *Price Tag (feat. B.o.B)*, Justin Timberlake - *Cry Me A River*, Pink - *Just Like A Pill*

chorus is a great technique because it gives you a chance to lyrically finish your story[1].

Instead of adding to the last chorus, it is also possible to *subtract hype from the third chorus.* This way you still get your precious rise in energy for the last chorus[2].

THE OUTRO.

This is the moment where John from our little movie earlier gets to meet his family again. It is a more personal ending that revolves around the character rather than the story. It simulates a return to the status quo. On the surface, it appears as though John is back where he started, but everything is different of course. Our hero has been through some life-changing events that have made him a stranger to his family.

The outro is a way of ending on a small and personal note. By rehashing the intro you come full circle, which can be used very effectively if you want to add a closed ending to your story. The main thing to keep in mind is to keep your outros short. This is the leave-them-

1 Staind - *Please,* Tina Dico - *The Other Side*
2 Sam Smith - *Stay With Me,* Linkin Park - *Until It's Gone*

wanting-more part. Do not keep this going longer than you absolutely have to.

OTHER WAYS TO END YOUR SONG

There are a lot of other options available to you that I want to quickly mention before we move on:

End On A Fade Out[1]. Even though fade outs are going out of fashion[2], this technique still pops up here and there in the charts every now and then. It suggests a kind of "and they lived happily ever after" - ending.

Ending Cold. This refers to ending with a big hit at the end or right after your finale. This can feel a little unsatisfying - It feels a little like watching Liam Neeson finally find and save his daughter in Taken and then not getting the satisfaction of seeing them be happy about it, but it has a lot of power.

---

1 Robin Thicke - *Blurred Lines,* Daft Punk - *Get Lucky,* Macklemore & Ryan Lewis - *Can't Hold Us (feat. Ray Dalton)*

2 Source: A Little Bit Softer Now, A Little Bit Softer Now - *The sad, gradual decline of the fade-out in popular music.. (article retrieved from www. slate.com)*

End On Another Post-Chorus. This will end your song on a groove. Why is this a great technique? Because like a pavlovian dog, the listener is subconsciously conditioned to think that after the post-chorus he will hear the verse again. If that doesn't happen, it's like they practically *have* to play your track again.

SUMMARY:

✓ The first verse introduces the song's theme and leads up to the chorus.

✓ The pre-chorus acts as a pivot point between verse and chorus. It needs to create tension.

✓ The first chorus should be the smallest of all choruses.

✓ The interlude is rhythm-based and acts as a soft landing from chorus to second verse.

✓ The second verse needs to be bigger than the first verse. Move forward!

✓ The second chorus should be slightly bigger than the first.

✓ The primary bridge should go into unexplored territory. Anything goes, as long as it leads up nicely into your finale.

✓ The third chorus is highly dependent on the fourth

and should thus be arranged after it.

✓ Ways to end your song: Outro, Fade Out, Cold Ending, Post-Chorus Ending

Alright. So you got an idea what the hollywood curve looks like and how it works. Now let's get to the good stuff, let's get practical. It's technique time.

PART 2: ELEMENTS

In this part you will learn everything you need to know about the six elements of songwriting:

✓ Arrangement   ✓ Part-Writing

✓ Harmony   ✓ Lyrics

✓ Rhythm   ✓ Production

INTRODUCTION TO PART 2
Now We're Talking

If music really is a language as many people say, then let's see what we can learn from communication that could be of interest to our writing process.

There are four steps to any form of communication: There is the conception of thought and encryption through language on your side, and a decryption and resulting thought or feeling on the side of your counterpart.

For example, a successful piece of communication on a first date would be:

Thought: *"I want us to get to know each other."*
Encryption: *"Did you know that I'm really into dinosaurs?"*

Decryption: *"She must really like dinosaurs"*
Thought: *"I now know something about her that I didn't know before. #communicationkicksass"*

…whereas communication gone wrong would be:

Thought: *"I want us to get to know each other."*
Encryption: *"Did you know that I'm really into dinosaurs?""*

___

Decryption: *"Oh my god, she has a weird fetish!"*
Thought: *"I am not a dinosaur and therefore not her type. #sad #tyrannosaurusex"*

In this case, the decryption part went wrong, which in turn might be because the encryption wasn't clear enough.

As songwriters, we face much the same problem: If one of the steps is not executed well, it will lead to confusion and most likely skepticism. The four steps translate to music as:

Thought: *The story you want to tell, i.e. your energy curve.*
Encryption: *Your finished production.*

___

Decryption: *How your audience perceives or understands your song.*
Thought: *How your audience likes or dislikes your song.*

We really can't control step number 4, but we can take control of steps 1 and 2 and if we do a good job with these, then step 3 will take care of itself.

Let's combine this idea with what we have learned so far:

✓ If you want your audience to understand you, you need something to communicate first. This statement does not necessarily have to be expressed through lyrics - music alone is perfectly capable of doing this, but your song needs intent, a *story*. As we have learned, this means playing with anticipation and gratification and choosing the right moments to switch between the two.

✓ This story can be expressed visually through energy curves. We have learned 9 paths our curve can take: *Jump, Smooth, Drop, Surprise, Overshoot, False Promise, Flatline, Lift* and *Negative Tension*.

✓ This curve is our starting point and all the elements of our song will follow it.

The next step is to express the energy curve in music. This can be seen as the encryption part of telling your story. As mentioned before, if your listener could draw your energy curve after listening to your song you did a good job encrypting. If however he draws a different, less musically beautiful curve, this means we failed in *telling* our story. The story itself might be fantastic, but if we can't express it through our music, it is practically worthless.

Part 2 of this book is all about telling your story. I call this process *riding the energy curve,* because if done right your song will take your listener on a ride[1]. We will go through each element of songwriting and see how it relates to your energy curve. Moving from the most general all the way down to the details, we will talk about the six elements of songwriting - arrangement, harmony, rhythm, part-writing, lyrics and production - and see how we can use each element to increase or decrease hype or introduce tension.

A COUPLE OF NOTES.

The following lists of techniques are by no means complete. My focus for this book was on commercial pop music, so if you write rock or country, I'm sure you can

---

1 This is also why I explain hype and tension as gears and gas.

think of more techniques to add to the chapters - and I openly invite you to do so! I am convinced that once you "get it" you can figure out where they belong and just scribble them in.

Measuring energy is not a precise science and it doesn't need to be. I've said it before but I want to say it again: Everything we will talk about is relative. If you play me a section of a song without letting me hear what comes before or after, it is impossible for me to determine how high in energy this section is.

The chapters of part II can be read out of order if you so desire. So if you're mostly interested in rhythm, you can jump there right now. I do however recommend reading the chapter on arrangement first because it contains a passage on *Implied Tension* which comes back in the other chapters.

It is important to understand that all the elements work together in a finished song. One element alone doesn't determine the look of your energy curve, it is rather the interplay of various elements acting at the same time. So even though one element in your song may go down in hype, the overall energy can still go up if another element increases in hype.

Remember: Not all techniques are equally powerful! Some barely change your energy and others can have a lot of impact. If you're ever in doubt which element is the most useful for what you're trying to accomplish, you can look it up on page 44. Or just listen.

ARRANGEMENT

When it comes to setting hype levels, there is no other element as powerful as arrangement. The art of deciding where certain instruments come in, what they play and when they drop out is one of the most important skills a songwriter could learn. And it's not just useful in theory: Literally every single song that has ever been a commercial success uses arrangement as its main tool to set hype levels.

So let's take what we learned when we studied energy curves and apply it here to find out what makes a successful arrangement:

- ✓ Give your song direction by increasing the hype level every 4 or 8 bars (this creates *anticipation*).
- ✓ Make your energy peaks (moments of *gratification*)

stand out above the rest of the song.

✓ Tension can be used to further smooth out transitions.

SETTING ENERGY LEVELS

So let's get down to the nitty gritty. The question is: how do we use arrangement to reflect our energy curve?

The rule is: The fuller the *texture*, the higher the hype.

Texture refers to the overall sound at a given moment during your song. So for example, a texture may consist of drums, a synth and a bass. To make things a little easier, we will start by looking at just the melodic instruments (drums are discussed separately in the chapter on part-writing), which we will divide into three frequency spectra:

Lows (bass, piano left hand bass),

Mids (piano left hand chords, rhythm guitar)

Highs (piano right hand, guitar higher up the neck)

So let's take each possible texture and put it in order from lightest (lowest hype) to fullest (maximum hype).

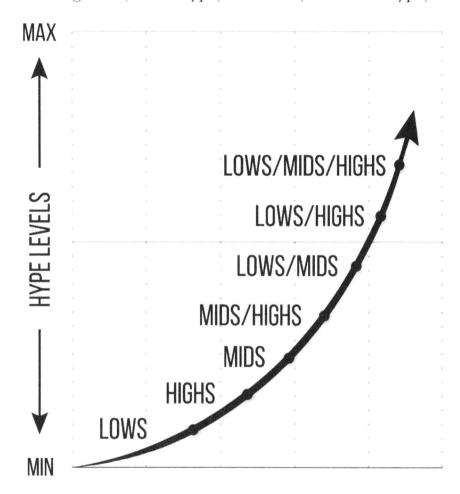

EXAMPLES.

None: Lorde - *Royals (intro)*, Avril Lavigne - Girlfriend (intro), Highs: Miley Cyrus - *We Can't Stop (first verse)*, Snow Patrol - *Chasing Cars (intro)*, Mids: Sam Smith - *Stay With Me (intro)*, Lows: Beyoncé - *Partition (interlude after first chorus)*, Mids/Highs: John Legend - *All Of Me (intro)*, Lows/Mids: Sam Smith - *Stay With Me*, Lows/Highs: Skrillex - *First Of The Year (Equinox, Chorus)*, Lows/Mids/Highs: Lady Gaga - *Venus (chorus)*, Katy Perry - *E.T. (chorus)*

So how can you use this graph? Well, if you're writing a song using just a piano and you want to increase your hype level, analyze what you are playing right now to see where you can go. So maybe you're playing high chords in the right hand and a low bass in the left. The only way to build hype through arrangement is filling out the middle. This could be done by using arpeggios in either hand to cover a wider range of pitches[1].

If you have more than one instrument, hype can also be increased by adding an instrument in the same frequency spectrum. While this won't make you very happy when mixing, you can create many more unique levels of hype this way.

---

1 Remember the days of stride patterns and pianists hitting high notes on the piano with their feet? That wasn't just energizing to watch, it also sounded like it.

The more textures you know and where they are on the hype spectrum, the more possibilities you have for telling your story. So study your favorite songs and listen to their textures - you can do just that. As long as you're using it in a new context, this is not stealing, it's *learning*.

USING TENSION

To introduce tension to a section, you have 2 options:

1. Thickening the texture, for example: adding an instrument half way through a section[1] or letting an instrument from the next part come in early[2].

2. Thinning out the texture. Taking out instruments in the middle of a section creates a hole in the music which wants to be filled in the next section[3], i.e. tension.

---

1 Awolnation - *Sail (section begins at 1:05, Pizzicato strings come in at 1:17)*, Clean Bandit - Rather Be *(section begins at 0:48, new bleepy sound comes in at 0:57)*, Staind - *Now (chorus starts a 16th note early)*
2 Clean Bandit - *Rather Be (piano pick-up at 1:03)*, Miley Cyrus - *Wrecking Ball (vocal pick-up at 0:41)*
3 Taylor Swift - *Blank Space (synth drops out before chorus 0:42)*, Katy Perry - *Dark Horse (feat. Juicy J, drums cut off at 1:24)*, Lorde - *Royals...*

IMPLY TENSION

The Third Kind Of Tension

There's a third option here which is a little bit harder to grasp. I'm talking about something I call *implied tension*. Learning how to use this kind of tension can be tricky, but is very rewarding. It is more subtle than straight-up tension and can be used to add interest to a section. Even though it is heavily featured in the top 200, not a lot of people know about it or use it in their songs.

Do you remember the last time you were angry with your significant other and for some reason you were stuck in the same room together? What did you do?

Maybe you confronted her. Told her exactly what you were thinking. Of course, she snaps back at you, you get back at her and both of you get louder and louder. It's loud, clear and straight to the point. This is regular tension.

(music drops out at 0:54), Seether - *Fine Again (One Cold Night, guitars drop out at 2:44, bass drops out at 2:48)*

But maybe you didn't fight it out. Maybe you just sucked up all your anger and gave each other the stinkeye. You know the feeling. Even though not a single word is being said, there is tension in the room. But it's not the same kind as when you were openly fighting. This is a subtle, conceived tension. When you could hear a pin drop - that's implied tension.

Structurally, implied tension is very different from regular tension because it is stationary. You don't look angrier and angrier at each other with every second. No, the tension comes from the fact that you are keeping quiet. Graphically, a section with implied tension looks like this:

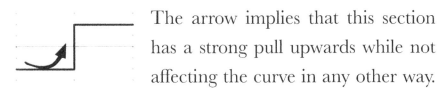

The arrow implies that this section has a strong pull upwards while not affecting the curve in any other way. Note that regular tension can be added to a section of implied tension, although technically it is not necessary (you're kind of putting a hat on a hat).

To really understand implied tension in music, listen to the following songs first and then we'll discuss it in full. For now, just try to feel the tension in the following sections.

Taylor Swift - *Blank Space (verse)*
Jason Derulo - *The Other Side (first verse)*
Deftones - *Sex Tape (0:43 - 0:54)*
Jhené Aiko - *The Worst (chorus)*
Tove Lo - *Habits, Hippie Sabotage Remix (0:48 - 1:03)*
XXYYXX - *About You (0:00 - 1:35)*
Avril Lavigne - *Girlfriend (opening chorus)*
Justin Bieber - *Beauty And A Beat (0:46 - 1:00)*

Can you feel how all these sections want to go somewhere? They all pull you towards the next section and thus mark moments of anticipation. And yet there's nothing building up or being taken away within the sections (If you didn't listen to the songs, do it now. Audition only one of them if you like, but experience it before you learn what it is).

Why do these arrangements sound tense? Let's look at them one by one and find out.

- There is a noticeable absence of bass in *Blank Space, Sex Tape, The Worst* (compared to the verses), *Girl-friend* and *About You*.
- The groove in *Sex Tape* is missing its bass drum. This is even more apparent in *Beauty And A Beat* where the side chain attenuates the space where the bass drum should be (called a *ghost kick*).
- The groove in *The Other Side* has no snare drum.
- The grooves of *Blank Space, The Worst* & *About You* leave a lot of space (no hi hat). *Girlfriend* does it too, but in a less obvious way (it's also not as tense).
- The vocals of *Habits* and *About You* sound tiny, the vocals in *Sex Tape* drop out completely.
- The pads in *Habits* build tension toward each hit of the snare drum, then instantly drop out.
- The guitars in *Girlfriend* play just one chord in the very beginning of the section and then keep mostly quiet.

So what do all of these have in common?

They make you notice that something is missing (bass, kick drum, snare drum, hi hat, vocals, pad, guitar). That's the key to writing implied tension. Give your listener a finger and they'll want the whole hand. What you are effectively doing is giving them a peek at the next moment of gratification by hinting at it during the anticipation phase. This makes implied tension a fantastic alternative to regular tension that is very "in"[1].

Another fascinating example of implied tension is A Perfect Circle's *Rose*. Listen to how it builds towards 0:37. This example is particularly interesting because it manages to keep the tension going for 3(!) consecutive sections.

Implied Tension is a little more complicated because it seems like a paradox at first: In order to build we have to thin out the arrangement - which is of course the exact opposite of how we use hype to increase energy.

So why is implied tension such a fantastic tool? Because it allows you to go down in hype while still keeping the listener hooked. There is no way around dropping your hype levels every now and then so you can build them back up again. This is where implied tension can really

---

1 Arrangements using a lot of implied tension: Kid Cudi vs Crookers - *Day 'n' Nite*, Iggy Azalea - *Fancy (feat. Charli XCX)*

shine. Take this rule as a guide line:

Whenever you use the Drop or Surprise (as discussed in *"The Perfect Energy Curve - Let's Go For A Ride"*), follow it up with some implied tension:

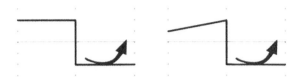

So again, the idea is to noticeably leave out an instrument, with an emphasis on "noticeably". If it's not noticeable, you're just going down in hype, which is always a tricky move to pull off.

SUMMARY:

- ✓ Hype can be altered by adding or subtracting elements from the frequency spectrum.
- ✓ Tension can be introduced by doing the same half way through a section.
- ✓ Implied Tension is a kind of tension that is based on noticeably stripping out elements of a section.

HARMONY

Harmony in commercial music has seen better days. I'm sure you've heard Axis of Awesome's *4 chords* and are already aware of this - what some might call - "problem". This is part of the reason why we will focus on triads and power chords in this book - no options, tensions, clusters or upper structures. If you are interested in how to use these chords with the Addiction Formula, I'm sure you can figure out how to apply them yourself after reading this chapter.

I'm assuming that you know basic harmony theory. In fact, I'm not intending to teach you anything new in this chapter but rather want to show you how you can use what you already know to tell your story, i.e. ride your energy curve.

SETTING HYPE

Chords, as any other songwriting element, can be used to set hype levels.

VOICINGS.

We already know this principle from the previous chapter on arrangement: The fuller the texture, the higher the hype. A wide voicing will lead to a higher hype level, a close voicing to a lower one. Refer to the graph in the arrangement chapter to determine how full your voicing is (p.107).

KEY CHANGES.

Changing the key for a new section is the most dramatic increase of hype possible in songwriting. It should be used very sparingly, so maybe once or twice on an album, because it is such a big move (you are *literally* moving your home). Where do you go? Up is the most popular choice, typically 1 or 2 half steps. 3 and 4 work and sound very dramatic, but anything more is pointless (and keep your singer's vocal range in mind).

Interestingly enough, the quality of a chord doesn't have any influence on hype. The chord's quality only becomes important when we look at tension:

USING TENSION

When I talked about tension in the very first chapter on building your energy curve, this is what probably popped into your head. And indeed, chords can be used very effectively to create tension.

First, let's decide which chords are of interest to us. The diagram on the opposite page displays the 10 most popular chords in hit songs[1].

To wrap our heads around tension, we begin by dividing a progression into 3 parts: A beginning, a middle and an end. We will start with the beginning, so we're looking at the first chord of a progression.

---

1 The percentages show the probability of whether a chord appears in a 4 or 8 bar section of a hit song (based on 1,300 analyzed songs). Source: www.hooktheory.com

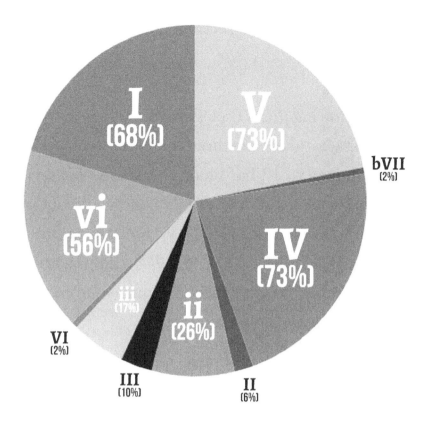

There are 3 types of starting chords that determine the feel of a section:

→ Tonic chords: *I, vi, iii, VI, III (major); i, VI, III (minor)*

→ Subdominant chords: *IV, ii, II (major); iv, IV (minor)*

→ Dominant chords: *V, bVII (major); V, VII, bII, v (minor)*

The category the first chord falls into determines how tense a section is: Dominant sections (thus sections that start with a dominant chord) are the most tense, followed by subdominant sections. Tonic sections have no natural tension.

Note: Knowing this is useless to you if you can't hear it. The best way to get the three categories into your head is by listening to 12-bar blues. It consists of 3 sections, one tonic, one sub-dominant and one dominant *(I - I - I - I, IV - IV - I - I, V - IV - I - V)*. So go listen to James Brown's *Papa's Got A Brand New Bag* and pay attention to how each 4 bars the tension changes - from tonic to subdominant to dominant.

EXAMPLES:

➤ Tonic section: I - iii - vi - IV, as in Jessie J's *Price Tag;*

➤ Subdominant section: IV - I - IV - I, as in Taylor Swift's *Mine (chorus);*

➤ Dominant section: V - IV - V - IV, as in Idina Menzel's *Let It Go (pre-chorus)*

The middle of a progression can also be used to introduce tension. This usually doesn't happen until the penultimate chord though, as shown in the following example:

I - IV - Vsus - V (suspended chord building tension towards dominant chord), *e.g. C - F - Gsus4 - G*

There are other ways to introduce tension earlier in a progression, although they are very rare in pop music. But just to be complete, here's two examples for progressions that build tension from the second chord onwards:

DOMINANT CHAINS
I - subV - V/V - V, *e.g. C - Eb7 - D7 - G7*

DESCENDING BASS LINES
i - i/maj7 - i/7 - i/6 - i/b6 - i/5 - V, *e.g. Cmin - Cmin/B - Cmin/Bb - Cmin/A - Cmin/Ab - Cmin/G - G*

The end of a progression is the most common place for creating tension. To build tension at the end of a progression, you want to use a concept known as *home and away*[1].

The I (in major) or vi (in minor) are your home, the

---

1 Kachulis, J - The Songwriter's Workshop: Harmony (Berklee Press, 2005)

chords with the lowest tension that your music keeps coming back to for resolution.

Everything else is *away* from home. How far away it actually is you can determine with the graph below. But the further you go, the more you build tension.

So here's our 10 most popular chords and how far from home they are:

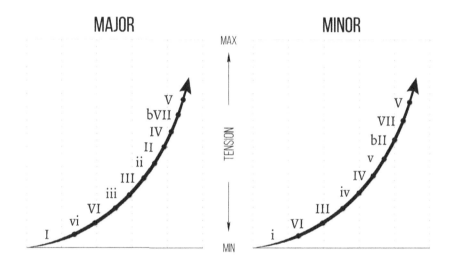

So, for example:

I - vi has very low tension.

vi - V has very high tension.

I - vi - IV - ii has medium tension.

I - IV - V - vi has very low tension.

IMPLY TENSION

Implied tension can be achieved by leaving out important notes of the chord, such as the root note (inversions) or the third (power chords). Note that leaving out a note has to be *noticeable* for it to imply tension. So for example, if you want to add implied tension to a section using power chords, make sure that the section right before it uses full triads.

That wraps up harmony for us. In the next chapter we will look at the most important element for creating tension with the Addiction Formula.

SUMMARY:

✓ Hype can be altered by the wideness of a voicing and through key changes.

✓ Tension can be introduced at the beginning, middle and end of a chord progression.

✓ Implied tension can be achieved by leaving out important notes of the chord, such as the root note (inversions) or the third (power chords).

RHYTHM

Rhythm is the most useful element for adding tension, period. Therefore, if you want to become a master songwriter, you absolutely have to be proficient in this. There is no good song without rhythm controlling hype and tension - literally not one! It is essential for your song to be captivating and to tell your story.

In order to understand how to set energy levels with rhythm, we first have to talk about subdivisions. There are 5 that are of interest to us:

> whole note or semibreve subdivision
> half note or minim subdivision
> quarter note or crotchet subdivision
> eighth note or quaver subdivision
> sixteenth note or semiquaver subdivision

The instrument that normally determines the subdivision is the drum kit because it's usually the instrument that plays the most notes[1].

In the remainder of this chapter, I will be referring to these as sub1, sub2, sub4, sub8 and sub16 in order to save paper and to keep everything short & neat.

SETTING HYPE

Let's look at our 5 subdivisions in terms of hype level:

SUBDIVISION DETERMINES HYPE.

The higher the subdivision, the higher the hype level, the lower the subdivision, the lower the hype. This is why songs often have their highest subdivision in the chorus and their lowest in the verse[2].

---

1 It doesn't have to be though. Listen to Britney Spears - *Work B**ch (subdivision given by guitar)* or Madonna - *Hung Up (subdivision given by synth)*

2 Sia - *Elastic Heart (1:10 - hi hat catapults song from sub8 to sub16, sub16 goes back to sub8 at 1:25)*

The more instruments following the highest subdivision, the higher the hype, the fewer instruments, the lower[1].

Note: Whenever you're trying to write a high-energy section, be aware that it's a balancing game between low and high subs. The lower subs bring power and heaviness to your song, whereas the higher subs bring in the energy.

Make a conscious decision of the effect you want to achieve and then react accordingly by tilting the balance towards either low or high subs:

MOSTLY LOW SUBS ←	→ BALANCE ←	→ MOSTLY HIGH SUBS
SLOW, RELAXED COOL, HEAVY	POWERFUL ENERGETIC	ENERGETIC BREATHLESS
JHENÉ AIKO - THE WORST RIHANNA - DISTURBIA	MUSE - HYSTERIA KATY PERRY - I KISSED A GIRL	MUTEMATH - SPOTLIGHT ALEX CLARE - UP ALL NIGHT

LEGATO TRUMPS STACCATO.

Switching from staccato to legato results in an increase

---

1 Sia - *Chandelier (0:23 - vocals start following subdivision)*, Justin Timberlake - *Cry Me A River (0:52 - vocals start following subdivision)*

of hype, going from legato to staccato lowers hype[1]. This is also why melodic lines always trump rap vocals in hype.

PHRASAL LENGTH.

To increase hype in this fashion, you want to shorten the length of your phrases[2]. Writing longer lines therefore lowers your energy level.

SWITCHING TO A HIGHER SUBDIVISION.

This is just as strong as leading up to the next section using dominant chains (and it doesn't sound as "old-fashioned"). Introducing a sub16 drum fill in a sub8 section is effectively telling your audience "but wait,

---

1 Some examples for vocals: Katy Perry - *E.T. (verse vs. pre-chorus)*, Sia - *Chandelier (pre-chorus vs. chorus)*, Lady Gaga - *Poker Face (verse vs. chorus vs. interlude)*, Jessie J - *Who's Laughing Now (verse vs. pre-chorus)*
2 Clean Bandit - *Rather Be (feat. Jess Glynne, phrasal acceleration in the vocals at 0:46)*, Far East Movement - *Like A G6 (0:15, "now I'm feeling so fly like a G6" shortens down to "like a G6")*

there's more"[1] by hinting at a higher level of hype.

IMPLY TENSION

BROKEN FLOW.

Again, implied tension is created by teasing the audience with something they want. In the case of rhythm, what your audience wants is continuous flow. So if you want to use implied tension, only let them have bits and pieces.

Check out Swift's *Blank Space* again: The verse is clearly in sub8 feel, but the vocals and drums suggest sub16. The point is that the vocals (and the drums especially) don't have satisfying sub16 lines, they just hint at it here and there.

Or listen to Beyoncé's *7/11:* The song is sub8, Beyoncé sings in sub16 and the hi hat even goes up to sub32 every now and then. This technique is very popular in trap music at the moment. A while ago, during the dubstep

---

1 Maroon 5 - *Moves Like Jagger (snare goes from sub8 to sub16 to sub32 at 1:32)*, Rihanna - *Rude Boy (snare going from sub8 to sub16 at 0:10)*.

craze, the implied tension came from the quarter note triplets in the bass trying to resolve into simple quarter notes. Again, the key is space. What you *aren't* saying is important.

CONTRARY MOVEMENT.

This one is a little more difficult to use, as it can easily clutter your arrangement. The idea is to let the drums fall in between the downbeats of the music. This way, you're creating a more "unexpected" drum beat that doesn't seem to hit when you want it to. This results in strong implied tension.

Listen to the second verse of Iggy Azalea's *Fancy* and imagine what it would sound like if the kick and snare would fall on the 1 and 3 of each measure. See how a lot of the implied tension goes right out the window?

SUMMARY:

✓ Hype can be controlled through change of the sub-division, by switching between legato and staccato and by playing with the phrasal length.
✓ Tension can be applied by switching to a higher subdivision half way through a section.

✓ Broken flow and contrary movement can be used to imply tension.

That wraps up rhythm for us. Now let's get to the individual parts of the instruments and see how they can be used to tell your story.

PART-WRITING

In this chapter, we will look at the five most common instruments - vocals, guitar, piano/synth, bass and drums - and see how they can be used to set hype levels and increase tension. If your favored musical instrument isn't among these, drop me an email and I will help you out.

Before we get all specific, I want to quickly go through a technique that works regardless of the instrument:

DYNAMICS.

Dynamics are one of the most important elements for controlling energy. In fact, just by looking at an energy curve, you can see the overall loudness at a glance. This just goes to show how closely connected dynamics and energy really are. It makes dynamics the easiest way of riding your energy curve.

If you've ever played in a band you will know that in the chorus everyone typically plays much louder than in a verse (*"You probably shouldn't stand so close to the drum set, man"* - *"Huh? I couldn't hear you, I'm standing too close to the drumset!"*). This is because every musician instinctively gets this. Because a wave's energy is proportional to amplitude squared, doubling your volume effectively *quadruples* your energy!

Hype. In order to set hype using dynamics, go louder for higher hype and softer for lower hype levels. This, of course, can also be achieved by adding another instrument in the arrangement.

Tension. Crescendos are your friend. Rising in volume automatically suggests that a big chorus will follow[1].

So just keep in mind that volume is a key element of your energy curve. Good. Let's take a look at our instruments.

---

1 The Calling - *Wherever You Will Go (0:41),* Beyoncé - *Yoncé/Partition (drums at 0:31),* Adele - *Set Fire to the Rain (drums at 0:55)*

1) VOCALS.

Think of ten purely instrumental songs that were hits in the past 40 years. Can't? Think of 5. How about 3? It seems that vocals are a necessary factor to writing a hit song. But are there other instruments that tend to get used a lot to replace the voice?

Electric guitars. Wonder why WahWah pedals are so popular in rock solos? Perhaps it sounds like the guitar is telling you what to think? Sounds like wow, wow, wow, doesn't it?

How many times have you heard people sing a dubstep bass line ("wob wob wob")? Does it vaguely sound like an angry "WHAT?" perhaps?

How about the saxophone? That had a huge career as a solo instrument in the 80s. It is also known as the instrument that is closest to the human voice.

Or take the harmon mute (that thing that makes a trumpet go "wah wah"), mimicking human laughter.

It appears that all the instruments that have ever made a hit song have one similar characteristic in common: Their closeness to the human voice.

What about classical music then? Classical singing is very different from what we hear on the radio of course. Upon comparing a violin's spectral analysis with a classical soprano's, Texas A&M biochemistry professor Joseph Nagyvary has found that sonically, they are practically the same. I don't know whether I am on to something here, but it seems like a strange coincidence, don't you think?

The human voice is undoubtedly important in arrangement. Sections without vocals are "just music"; it's only when the human voice is involved that the song begins to speak to us.

Listen to Katy Perry's *Dark Horse (feat. Juicy J)*: There is not a single section in this song where we don't hear some form of the human voice. Even the instrumental interlude after the first chorus has "hey"s in the background[1]. If you want high energy, think of ways to incorporate the human voice into every section of your song.

Most of the following techniques can also be used for other melodic leads, such as guitar, saxophone or synth solos.

RANGE.

Controlling hype with vocals is mostly done by pitch: The higher the pitch, the higher the hype; the lower the pitch, the lower the hype. This is the reason why most songs have their highest notes in the chorus and their lowest in the verse[2].

---

1 A sample known as *mustard hey* - on its way to becoming music's Wilhelm Scream.

2 Miley Cyrus - *Wrecking Ball*, Lady Gaga - *Poker Face*, Rihanna - *S&M*, Pink - *Raise Your Glass*

VARIETY.

The more different notes, the higher the hype. This means one-note melodies have the lowest hype[1].

VOCAL MODES.

There are several schools of vocal technique out there using their own definitions and nomenclature[2] and the more you know about the instrument you're writing for, the better. However, it is unusual to ask a singer to lower her larynx in the studio. It's better to know a couple of *sounds* that are possible with the voice and trust the singer to produce said sound. This approach works regardless of the education the singer has gone through. So as far as I'm concerned, there are 4 sounds you need to be aware of:

Neutral, Falsetto (aka *Neutral with Air*) and *Speech*, which turns into *Belting* (aka *Edge*) at higher pitches. And here are their hype levels, taking pitch into consideration:

---

1 Lady Gaga - *Poker Face (one-note melodies in verses, most different notes in chorus)*

2 Cathrine Sadolin's *Complete Vocal Technique* (CVT) and Jo Estill's *Estill Voice Training* (EVT) being the most widely taught.

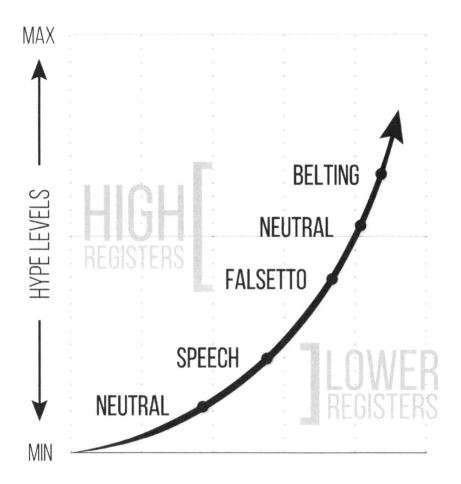

EXAMPLES.

Belting: Miley Cyrus - *Wrecking Ball (chorus)*, Sia - Chandelier *(chorus)*; Neutral (high): John Legend - *All Of Me (1:32 - 1:43)*, Ariana Grande - *Problem (feat. Iggy Azalea)*; Falsetto: Katy Perry - *E.T. (pre-chorus)*, *Dark Horse (pre-chorus)*, Britney Spears - *Toxic (pre-chorus)*; Speech: Ke$ha - *TiK ToK (chorus)*, Katy Perry - *E.T. (verse)*, Lady

Gaga - *Poker Face ("po-po-po-poker face, po-po-poker face")*; Neutral (lower): One Republic - *Counting Stars (verse)*, Lorde - *Royals*

EFFECTS.

There is also a multitude of effects that can be added on top of the vocal modes to create more interesting colors and control energy:

Twang (Oral & Nasal). Hype can be raised by adding twang to a vocal[1]. Since it's a requirement for belting, twang is often associated with high-energy choruses, although it can be used in any kind of section[2].

Vibrato. This effect is often added to long notes in order to create interest. Especially in ballads we hear it quite often[3]. By effectively adding more rhythmic pulses to a line, vibrato makes for another technique that can be used to increase hype[4].

---

1 Lady Gaga - *Bad Romance (twang sets in at 0:17)*

2 Miley Cyrus - *We Can't Stop*, Pink - *Raise Your Glass*, Rihanna - *Umbrella*

3 Beyoncé - *If I Were A Boy*, John Legend - *All Of Me*

4 Beyoncé - *Listen*, Ariana Grande - *Break Free (feat. Zedd)*

Ornamentations. This little technique (CVT describes it as *"A technique used for producing very fast, rhythmic, and melodic sequences of notes."*[1]) is often used in RnB[2]. Since it increases the amount of sung pitches (*Variety*) and notes (*Rhythm*), this clearly adds hype.

Distortion. Apart from very subtle kinds (known as *Curbing*[3]), pop music doesn't see a lot of distortion. In alternative rock and metal we see other, more extreme types that can be classified by pitch. The lowest in hype is known as *Growling*[4] (low pitch), followed by the mid-ranged *Shouting*[5] and the high-pitched *Screaming*[6] (highest hype).

---

1 Extracted from *http://completevocalinstitute.com/cvtresearchsite/ornamentation-technique/*

2 Ariana Grande - *Problem ft. Iggy Azalea (2:46 - end)*

3 Mr Probz - *Waves,* Nickelback - *How You Remind Me*

4 Opeth - *The Grand Conjuration (1:06),* Six Feet Under - *Ghosts Of The Undead,* Arch Enemy - *War Eternal*

5 Slayer - *Bloodline,* Sepultura - *Roots Bloody Roots,* Pantera - *Walk*

6 Refused - *New Noise (0:43),* Linkin Park - *One Step Closer (2:06),* Neaera - *Let The Tempest Come,* Bring Me The Horizon - *Can You Feel My Heart*

USING TENSION

WRITE ASCENDING MELODIES,

i.e. melodies that rise in pitch[1]. As pitch determines hype, it only makes sense that slowly increasing pitch introduces tension. Vice versa, you can use descending melodies to create negative tension, which is something often seen when transitioning from chorus to verse[2].

CHANGE THE VOCAL MODE.

For this technique, you want to instruct your singer to change their sound to one with more hype in the middle of the section[3]. It is also possible to amplify the intensity by telling the singer to slowly increase her singing power[4].

---

1 Katy Perry - *Firework (0:39 - 0:54)*, Sierra Swan - *Sex Is Keeping Us Together (0:31 - 0:43)*, Ariana Grande - *Problem (feat. Iggy Azalea, 0:30 - 0:39)*, Taio Cruz - *Dynamite (0:24 - 0:32)*

2 Clean Bandit - *Rather Be (feat Jess Glynne, 2:51)*

3 Katy Perry - *Dark Horse (feat. Juicy J, Falsetto to Neutral at 0:34)*, Fall Out Boy - *Dance, Dance (0:39, neutral to belting)*

4 Natasha Bedingfield - *Soulmate (2:16)*

HITTING TENSE NOTES.

For example, you might hit the 3rd or 7th of a V chord during the end of a section. This tension technique is not seen a lot in pop music these days because it immediately sounds classical or clichéd. Hitting these notes highlights the underlying harmony, which - as we have learned - is kind of "out" as a means to create tension.

CREATING TENSION WITH EFFECTS.

By slowly adding twang or distortion to a voice you are signalling that you're moving to a section with higher energy[1]. Vibrato is rarely used for doing this anymore, maybe because it sounds a little too Freddy Mercury for this century.

Vocals are a great tool for introducing implied tension to your song because everyone is focused on them. Here's four techniques you can use:

---

1 Pink - *Raise Your Glass (1:32 - first twang, then distortion)*, Clean Bandit - *Rather Be (feat. Jess Glynne, 3:07 twang)*, Element Eighty - *Goodbye (0:25 distortion)*

SUBTRACT THE MELODY.

Since the human voice is the part that has most of your audience's attention, taking out the vocals has a lot of impact. Right before the chorus is the most popular choice to do this[1].

WRITE A TENSE ONE-NOTE MELODY.

Pick a note for your one-note melody that isn't part of your tonic triad. This creates a nice friction between vocals and music which wants to resolve, i.e. implied tension[2].

THE FINAL FRONTIER: SPACE.

By space I mean a period of time between two lines before a pause turns into a rest. Not using space in their melodies is one of the biggest issues songwriters have; their verses are just a huge block of text. I call this phenomenon *lyrical chains.* Making a lyrical chain groove is truly a hard thing to do[3].

---

1 Lady Gaga - *Applause (0:53)*

2 Justin Timberlake - *Pose (feat. Snoop Dogg, verses on 11)*, Janelle Monáe - *Tightrope (verses on b7)*

3 Shakira - *Whenever, Wherever*, Beyoncé - *Run The World (Girls)*, Justin Timberlake - *Pose*

The best melodies say what they need to say in as little words as possible. This allows the song to breathe (literally) and lets the music shine through every once in a while. This is especially important in ballads. Bryan Adams is a master at this, as you can hear in *Where Angels Fear To Tread* and *Inside Out.* Listen to how he sings literally as little as possible. Take out one note and it doesn't work anymore. Just for fun, take *Inside Out* and continue his melody, fill up the space between his lines. Can you feel how that completely destroys the tension of the song? I dare you to write something better with more words[1].

The success of this technique is greatly dependent on the performer: Your singer needs to be able to turn rests into space. This has a lot to do with breath and tension in the voice itself. The best way to accomplishing this is by making sure they sing your lyrics in blocks, not line-by-line.

---

1 For more recent examples, listen to Lady Gaga - *Applause,* The Script - *Breakeven,* A Great Big World & Christina Aguilera - *Say Something*

ATTITUDE.

Tension can also be implied by contrasting music with a different energy in the vocals. Low-energy vocals set to high-energy music can reflect powerlessness, boredom, apathy or depression[1]. Setting high-energy vocals to low-energy music can be used for super-emotional ballads or whenever we want the singer's vocal abilities to stand out[2].

SUMMARY:

✓ Hype levels can be expressed through loudness, range, variety, the four vocal modes (neutral, falsetto, speech and belting) and effects (twang, vibrato, ornamentations, distortion).

✓ To introduce tension, use crescendos, ascending melodies, change the vocal mode, hit tense notes or gradually add effects.

✓ Implied tension can be achieved by subtracting the melody, by writing a tense one-note melody, by using space or by attitude.

---

1 Stromae - *Alors On Danse*, The Cranberries - *Zombie*, Katatonia - *Soil's Song*, Deftones - *Be Quiet And Drive (Far Away)*

2 Ed Sheeran - *Thinking Out Loud*, Adele - *Someone Like You*, Christina Aguilera - *Hurt*, Beyoncé - *Listen*, Staind - *Pardon Me*

2) GUITAR.

SETTING HYPE

As with vocals, there are a lot of different techniques on the guitar that can be utilized to set hype levels.

Most of the techniques used by vocals can be directly translated to writing guitar parts (and all other melodic instruments for that matter). What is often overlooked though is that the overall level of hype is already determined before the first note is struck: I'm talking about picking styles here:

While they influence the general hype level, a guitarist usually doesn't switch picks during a song, so knowing this is of limited use for riding the energy curve. In the acoustic guitar world however, switching from fingers to pick half way through a song is quite common and can thus be used as a tachnique to set different hype levels as well.

So whether you're interested in raising the general hype level or riding the energy curve, it's good to know that there are plenty different sizes and shapes to go with and what influence they have on your energy - it's your pick[1]:

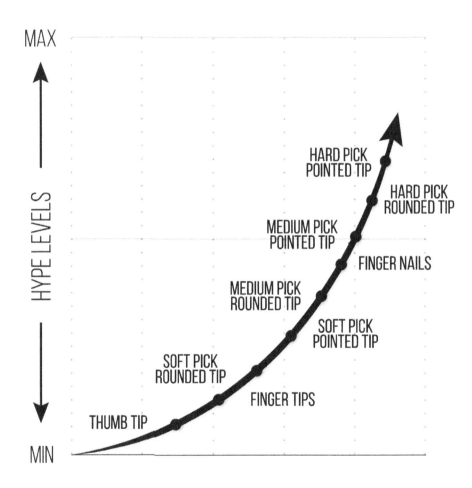

---

1 The world needed another pick joke.

GUITAR MODES.

The biggest influence a guitarist has on hype is through what they actually play:

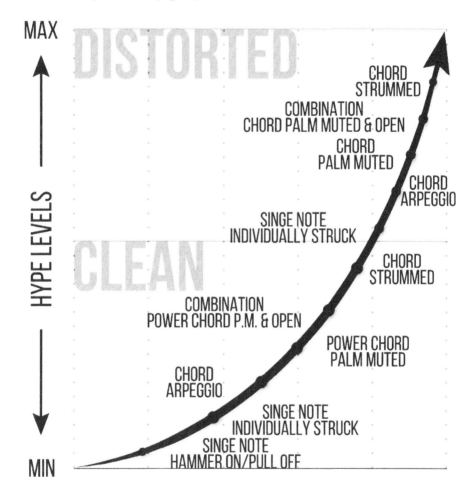

EXAMPLES.

DISTORTED: Chord (Strummed): Linkin Park - *Crawling (chorus);* Combination Chord Palm Muted &

Open: Green Day - *Basket Case (first verse)*, Fall Out Boy - *Thnks fr th Mmrs (second verse)*; Chord (Palm Muted): Avril Lavigne - *Sk8er Boi (verse)*, Element Eighty - *War*; Chord Arpeggio: Bryan Adams - *C'mon, C'mon, C'mon (chorus)*; Single Notes (Individually Struck): Sum 41 - *We're All To Blame (intro)*;

CLEAN: Chord Strummed: Oasis - *Wonderwall*; Combination Power Chord Palm Muted & Open: Seether - *Love Her (verses)*; Power Chord (Palm Muted): Avril Lavigne - *I'm With You (Verse)*, Wheatus - *Teenage Dirtbag (prim. bridge)*; Chord Arpeggio: Pink - *Sober (verse)*, Avril Lavigne - *Nobody's Home (intro)*; Single Notes (Individually Struck): System Of A Down - *Toxicity (intro)*; Single Notes (Hammer On / Pull Off): Bryan Adams - *C'mon, C'mon, C'mon (intro)*.

Listen to Steve Vai's *Tender Surrender* for a moment[1] - I know, that hair! - to hear a lot of these in action, including thumb tip (0:33), nail (0:42) and pick playing (1:22). Notice how subtly he switches between clean and distorted sounds (2:00, 3:57)? How he controls hype by going through various dynamics, subdivisions, ranges and playing styles?

---

1 You can find it on Steve's youtube channel *SteveVaiHimself*.

This performance showcases Steve's true mastery of energy, slowly building towards his moment of gratification in the middle of the piece and slowly going back down again.

EFFECTS.

We will discuss effects when we talk about Producing, because they too can be used to express our energy curve.

USING TENSION

Tender Surrender also uses pretty much all types of tension that are possible on guitar: *Palm mutes (1:47),* different kinds of *vibrato (clean 1:25, distorted 2:03 & 2:37, tremolo bar vibrato 2:53, 3:30), tremolo bar drops (3:06)* and *squeals (3:14), slow bends (3:34), pick slides (3:53).* The only ones missing are the *slide, harmonics, fades* and the *chug*[1].

---

1 Eminem - *Cleanin' Out My Closet (slide at 1:12),* Linkin Park - *Crawling (harmonics at 0:25),* Evanescence - *Bring Me To Life (fade at 0:28),* Avril Lavigne - *Losing Grip (chug at 2:43)*

One playing style that is particularly interesting for creating tension on guitar is palm muted playing. Resting the flesh of his hand on the strings, the guitarist can control how much he wants to mute the strings. By slowly taking off the hand, a natural crescendo occurs and the sound becomes more open and legato[1]. This is the exact equivalent to slowly opening a hi hat on drums.

Note that once a guitar is distorted, its dynamic capabilities are very limited due to the compression of the distortion. Using palm mute crescendos is an excellent way of making up for this shortfall.

PALM MUTES.

Palm mutes also sound great when kept closed. They sound very thick and abrupt and can be used to create implied tension[2].

1 System Of A Down - *Toxicity (build-up to chorus, around 1:13)*
2 Deftones - *You've Seen The Butcher (intro)*

SLIDES.

Slides can also be used to imply tension if used multiple times in one section[1].

DRONES.

This is especially popular in metal and ethnic music. Here, the guitarist structures their riffs around a low open string (similar to a *pedal*). This sounds very sinister and dark but can have some very hypnotic qualities[2].

SUMMARY:

✓ Hype can be altered through dynamics, picking styles, guitar modes, range, variety and effects.

✓ Tension can be introduced by using crescendos, palm mutes, vibrato, tremolo bar drops, squeals, slow bends, pick slides, slides, harmonics, fades and the chug.

✓ To imply tension, use palm mutes, slides or drones.

---

1 Limp Bizkit - *Rollin' (verse & chorus)*

2 Deftones - *Sex Tape (verse)*, Tool - *Vicarious (e.g. 2:47)*

3) BASS

SETTING HYPE

BASS MODES.

Let's look at the hype levels first:

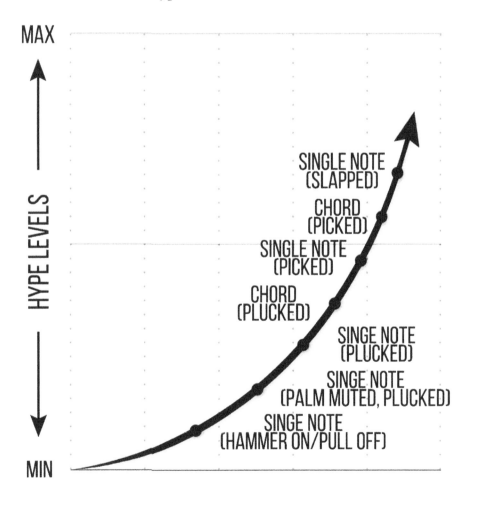

EXAMPLES.

Slap: OutKast - *Ms. Jackson (0:43),* Jordin Sparks - *One Step At A Time (chorus);* Chord Picked: Red Hot Chili Peppers - *Don't Forget Me;* Single Note Picked: Alex Clare - *Up All Night;* Chord (Plucked): Red Hot Chili Peppers - *Hey;* Single Note Plucked: Robin Thicke - *Blurred Lines (feat. T.I. & Pharrell);* Single Note (Palm Muted & Plucked): MAGIC! - *Rude;* Single Note (Hammer On / Pull Off): Red Hot Chili Peppers - *Around The World*

DISTORTION

Distortion adds a whole new level to these hype levels, meaning that even the highest clean hype level doesn't sound as big as the lowest distortion level.

The bass is a little more limited when it comes to tension as most of the techniques discussed in the chapter on guitar don't sound as good on thick strings. The most common technique of creating tension is the slide[1].

---

1 Red Hot Chili Peppers - *Scar Tissue (0:10)*

SLIDES.

Just as on guitar, using slides multiple times in a section can be used to imply tension[1].

DRONES.

By playing a continuous drone some of your chords will start creating friction. This technique can thus be used very effectively to imply tension[2].

SUMMARY:

✓ Hype can be controlled through dynamics, range, variety, changing bass modes and distortion.

✓ Tension can be added by using crescendos or slides.

✓ To imply tension, slides or drones can be used.

---

1 Pharrell Williams - *Marilyn Monroe (verse)*

2 Katy Perry - *I Kissed A Girl (chorus)*, Mudvayne - *Pulling The String (intro)*, Portishead - *Machine Gun*

4) PIANO & SYNTHESIZERS

Compared to the other instruments, the piano is the most neutral when it comes to energy. It really only has one sound - that of a hammer striking a string. So we will include synths in this chapter as well.

We have already discussed the most important hype features of the piano in other parts of this book. They are dynamics (page 131), ranges (page 135) and rhythm (page 124) .

SUSTAIN.

The only popular instrument-specific technique of the piano is using the sustain pedal: It opens up the sound and thus lifts the section to a new hype level.

FILTERS.

The hype of synthesizers can often be set with low pass filters - the lower the cut-off, the lower the hype.

USING TENSION

There is no tension on piano. I've heard some alternative tracks where the sustain pedal was held in order to blend successive chords, thereby creating some sort of cluster chords, but it is a rarity.

In the case of synthesizers, the cut-off frequency of the low-pass filter can be automated to slowly open up[1].

SUMMARY:

✓ Hype can be controlled by means of dynamics, range, variety, sustain and filters.

✓ Tension can be applied by changing the cut-off frequency of the filter.

---

1 Ariana Grande - *Break Free (feat. Zedd, first verse),* Jennifer Lopez - *Live It Up (feat. Pitbull, intro)*

5) DRUMS

Drums are your most powerful instrument for controlling energy, period. They like no other can set your hype levels and introduce tension, so studying groove is extremely valuable for any songwriter. Bringing in drums half-way through a song is one of the most impactful moves in the world of songwriting ever since Led Zeppelin's *Stairway To Heaven* and Phil Collin's *In The Air Tonight*. So let's talk instruments. There are 4 parts a drummer can play simultaneously, one for each limb (2 legs, 2 arms). This translates to:

LEFT ARM: **SNARE**   RIGHT ARM: **TIME**

LEFT LEG: **HAT PEDAL**   RIGHT LEG: **KICK**

Obviously, there are more possibilities than these if you take patterns played with both hands, not to mention special pedals into account, but as you will see, this won't really matter for our discussion. This is because we are not interested in the amount of notes played on an instrument in this chapter (we covered this in the chapter on rhythm), just which instruments we can hear in general.

SETTING HYPE

DRUM MODES.

At the moment, we are only discussing "full" beats, meaning beats involving a kick drum, snare drum and time in the right hand. To be more specific, we are especially interested in the right hand, because it will determine our hype level the most.

So here are the different hype levels on drums you need to know as an arranger:

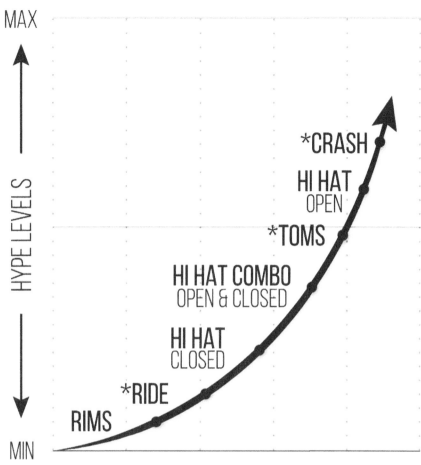

MAX

HYPE LEVELS

*CRASH

HI HAT
OPEN

*TOMS

HI HAT COMBO
OPEN & CLOSED

HI HAT
CLOSED

*RIDE

RIMS

MIN

*rare in pop music

EXAMPLES.

Crash: Sum 41 - *Fatlip (chorus);* Hi Hat (Open): Sia - *Elastic Heart (first half of chorus),* Foo Fighters - *The Pretender (second verse);* Toms: Sia - *Clap Your Hands,* P.O.D. - *Youth Of The Nation (chorus),* System Of A Down - *Chop Suey (intro);* Hi Hat Combo (Open & Closed): Pink - *So-*

ber (chorus); Hi Hat (Closed): Justin Timberlake - *What Goes Around... Comes Around,* Usher - *Climax (verse),* Sum 41 - *Fatlip (verse);* Ride: Foo Fighters - *The Pretender (chorus),* KoRn - *Blind (intro);* Rims: Alex Clare - *Too Close (verse)*

Intermediate steps can be reached by involving an instrument that's higher in hype, e.g. an open hi hat beat with an added crash has a higher hype level than without the crash. Adding instruments from a lower hype level usually sounds weak, e.g. playing a tom groove and adding a ride on the downbeat. This rule does not include fills or any other type of tension building, of course.

RIMS.

There are two other important sounds on the snare drum that have an influence on hype: The rim click (a.k.a. cross stick or side stick) and the rim shot. The rim click lowers the hype level of the drum groove, the rim shot increases it.

SNARES OFF.

This way of playing is often heard in Raggae music. With the snares disengaged, the snare drum sounds more like a tom-tom, which dramatically decreases its hype level. This can be compared to going from distorted guitar to clean guitar. Using the snares to set hype levels is rarely used in pop music, but very musical and effective[1].

USING TENSION

CHANGING MODES.

Tension again may be achieved by either involving new instruments half way through a section such as fills on toms, crashes, snare rolls, cymbal rolls[2] or by dropping out the drums entirely[3]. Another great way is to gradually open the hi hat or to gradually move from the bell of the ride outwards (going from a "ping" sound to a washed out crash sound)[4].

---

1 Mr Probz - *Waves (snares on at 1:18)*

2 Junkie XL - *A Little Less Conversation (feat. Elvis, tom fill at 1:26)*, JAY Z & Alicia Keys - *Empire State of Mind (crashes at 1:06)*, B.o.B - *Airplanes ft. Hayley Williams (snare fill at 0:29)*, Sean Paul - *Got 2 Luv U... (feat. Alexis Jordan, cymbal roll at 1:35)*, Eminem - *Till I Collapse (cymbal roll at 0:27)*

3 Lorde - *Team (drums drop out at 1:02)*, B.o.B - *Airplanes (feat. Hayley Williams, drums drop out at 0:51 & 1:09)*

4 Limp Bizkit - *Rollin (hi hat starts opening at 0:17)*, Finger Eleven - ...

IMPLY TENSION

We have already talked about a multitude of ways of creating implied tension in the arrangement section of this book. The basic rule is: Give your audience only part of what they want. In the case of the drums, this translates to giving them an incomplete beat that is missing either its bass drum, snare drum, time or combinations of the three.

There are 3 additional grooves I want to briefly mention that imply tension to your music:

HALF-OPENED HI HAT.

We are so used to the sound of the hi hat gradually opening up - thus going somewhere - that we instinctively associate the sound with tension, even if the hat doesn't actually open up any further.

Paralyzer (hi hat opens at 0:50)

TOM GROOVES.

These we know primarily from drum solos - and since those always end with a big bang our anticipation is high here as well.

SNARE DRUM GROOVES AND ROLLS.

These work for similar reasons as the previous[1]. They feel like a long snare drum fill. It's not a coincidence that snare drum rolls are used in circuses to introduce tension. We all know that at the end of the roll the lion will jump the hoop. Weird, innit?

SUMMARY:

✓ Hype can be altered through dynamics, variety, drum modes, rims and by disengaging the snares.

✓ Tension can be applied by changing modes or through crescendos.

✓ To imply tension, use half-opened hi hat grooves, tom grooves or snare drum grooves and rolls.

---

1 Ke$ha - *Die Young (snare drum grooves at 0:22 and 0:30)*, Linkin Park - *Until It's Gone (snare drum roll at 1:01)*, Mr Probz - *Waves (snare drum roll at 0:56)*, Beyoncé - *Run The World (Girls, combinations of snare drum grooves and rolls throughout the entire song)*

So we've talked about arrangement, harmony, rhythm and part-writing. Now it's time to take a look at lyrics and how they can be used to represent your energy curve.

LYRICS

Music and lyrics are not separate entities. Lyrics - just like any other element of songwriting - are a tool to control your energy curve. We have already discussed the important role of vocals in hit songs, now it's time to look at what these vocals could be singing about and - even more importantly - *how* they sing about it.

Just like all the other elements, lyrics have periods of anticipation and moments of gratification. In other words, they, too, can be used to set hype levels and build tension.

Another key mistake writers make is that they write their music and lyrics independently. This is not a problem per se, but it becomes a problem if their energy levels don't match up. Music and lyrics need to follow the same energy curve or they will not fit.

EXAMPLES.

Take a look at the following (unrelated) lines:

Shut up and listen to me
Everybody put your hands up
I met her at a concert
His hands wrinkled and grey

See how these have different hype levels? The first two lines would sound really strange in a section of low hype and the last two wouldn't work in a high-energy setting.

The primary bridge of Rebecca Black's *Friday* ("Yesterday was thursday...") is a great unintentional example for energy levels not matching up. Here, the tension builds and builds whereas the lyrics peter out in banalities. It's the equivalent of a clown riding a tiny bike.

Having different elements of your song say different things is a huge trap to fall into. Make sure your music and lyrics tell the same story and start seeing lyrics as a part of the music instead of as a separate entity[1]. Start seeing lyrics as simply another instrument that has different sounds and techniques you can use to alter your energy curve.

Before we get into how to set hype and tension, there is a concept we need to talk about that becomes very important in lyric writing:

POWER POSITIONS.

Certain moments in your song provide better opportunities for storytelling than others. These moments are called *power positions* because they give whatever lyric is there higher status.

So where are those power positions? The most obvious are choruses and highest overall notes. They are the most impactful and memorable moments of your song, so it only makes sense to put some fantastic lines here.

But what about the rest of the song? Are there other less obvious power positions we can use? The answer

---

1 In fact, having music and lyrics go in completely different directions is a great technique if you do comedy. Weird Al, anyone?

goes back to the Golden Mean.

A quick reminder: The golden mean or 1-2-3 rule says that after you have introduced something, repeat it once, then change it. Why can we use this rule here? Because it shows the critical moments of change in our song and change always calls attention to the music. That means that the lines in these positions are more valuable than others. So let's look at one of these golden mean lines here:

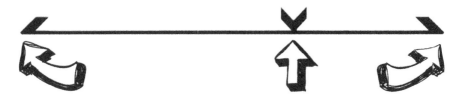

Notice that it has a three distinct features: A beginning, a mark at around two thirds of the distance between the two and an end. These 3 moments (*nodes*) are power positions - they either introduce a new section, introduce something new or round off the section. So in a verse - verse - pre-chorus scenario, your power positions are the first line of the verse, the last line of the verse (or the first line of the pre-chorus) and the last line of the pre-chorus:

VERSE VERSE **PRE**

Let's look at our hollywood structure as an example:

PRE **CHORUS** PRE **CHORUS** BRIDGE BRIDGE **CHORUS**

According to this, the power positions are:

> First line of first verse
> First line of pre-chorus / last line of first verse
> First line of first chorus / last line of pre-chorus
> First line of second verse / last line of first chorus
> First line of second chorus / last line of pre-chorus
> First line of prim. bridge / last line of second chorus
> First line of last chorus / last line of prim. bridge
> Last line of last chorus

But the little graph above also shows us which power positions are the most valuable. Looking at how many nodes coincide in one place, it becomes obvious that the most powerful position is the first line of the primary bridge / last line of the second chorus (with 3 nodes). This is followed by the very first and very last line of the lyrics (2 nodes). In other words, these lines happen at the most memorable and spectacular moments of your song and thus provide the best opportunity for a strong line.

So we have identified our strongest power positions (and using the 1-2-3 rule is an excellent way of doing this if you're ever in doubt about a structure), now it's time to talk about how to make the best use of them.

SETTING HYPE

It should be said that lyrics have only little influence on a song's hype level. Unless you use extremely powerful words, they will usually adapt more or less to your songs energy curve.

But anyways, setting hype through lyrics is done by using *scope* and *power words*.

Scope refers to how specific or general something is. Specificity is low hype, big picture stuff is high hype. If specificity is what you want, describe what you see or what you feel as something's happening. Go into detail, talk about the smaller things in life, tell a story. If you want to go big, explain, summarize, reveal. Go meta[1].

Power Words can be used to raise hype. Songwriters are always on the lookout for these. Madonna did it with the word "virgin", Beyoncé did it with "ring" and Lady Gaga did it with "paparazzi". All of these are words either evoke a strong emotional reaction (anything from "you can't say *that*! what are the kids gonna think?" to "that sums up exactly how I feel") or have a deeper meaning (Beyoncé's "ring" is a metaphor for marriage and honesty). Power words can also reflect the artist's image[2] or the zeitgeist[3].

Have you heard of Pareto's principle? 20% of your efforts produce 80% of your results. Your power words are those 20%! People will forget the rest of your lyrics, but power words prevail. So when writing lyrics, spend

1 Beyoncé - *Single Ladies (verse: specific, chorus: explanation)*, Big Sean - *Beware (feat. Lil Wayne & Jhené Aiko, verses: specific, chorus: message)*
2 "Single ladies" reads girl power, Gaga's "poker face" is used synonymously with playing hard to get
3 Katy Perry - *I kissed a girl (LGBT movement)*, Lady Gaga - *G.U.Y. (bottom power, feminism)*, Beyoncé - *XO (generation of internet relationships)*, Wheatus - *Teenage Dirtbag (high school)*, Bee Gees - *Night Fever (disco era)*

more time on your key power words than on anything else. Judging from the lyrical quality of the verses of even hit songs, this is what the pros do, too. Put power words in power positions and your lyric will become irresistible.

USING TENSION

This is where lyrics really can shine. Since they are the only element that can tell a literal story, all the same techniques can be used for creating tension as in poetry, novels and screenplays.

There are two big ways in which to work some tension into your lyrics: *Contentual Tension* and the less known, although much more effective *Structural Tension*.

CONTENTUAL TENSION

This type of tension has to do with what you're saying. Since it is purely logical (your listener has to make an effort to follow and understand the lyrics), it isn't as strong as Structural Tension. Since it's not used a lot in pop music, we will go through this rather quickly.

Telling A Story. This technique is a little dated. It pops up here and there every once in a while, especially in country and folk music but is rarely seen in pop. Examples might be Eminem's *Stan*, Paramore's *Brick By Boring Brick*, Flyleaf's *Cassie* or Alanis Morissette's *Your House*. This approach to writing lyrics is more textbook than practice, almost to a degree where there are more books on the technique than hits actually using it. It can be a lot of fun though and is one of the more inspiring methods for writing lyrics (compared to "let's think of more ways to tell my boyfriend he's special without sounding sappy or corny").

Cliffhangers. Cliffhangers are a technique borrowed from TV writing where you either introduce a major change of events ("He was a horse the whole time!"), a question ("How did he know we were coming?") or cut off a chain of events ("The secret of Blackmoore castle lies behind this door. Let's open it next week!") at the end of the episode to make sure people tune in again.

The same thing can be done with lyrics: You are looking for lines that are going somewhere, lines that build tension. So find a line that either surprises (high tension)[1], creates interest[2] (medium tension) or leads nicely into the next section[3] (low tension).

STRUCTURAL TENSION

Traditionally, lyrics are written in blocks of 4 lines each, with one block per section. This is usually a pretty safe technique that helps with rhyming and flow.

The problem with this approach is that blocks are predictable: We know when they start, we know when they end and we know there's gonna be another block just like it right after. Writing in blocks has a certain sound that, if not used with care, can sound cliché, flat or one-dimensional.

The following techniques can help you loosen up your block writing in order to introduce some structural tension to your lyrics.

---

1 Prim. Bridges of Beyoncé's *If I Were A Boy* and *Single Ladies (Put A Ring On It)*
2 First lines of Katy Perry's *Unconditionally*
3 Last lines of the verses in Eminem's *Monster (feat. Rihanna)*

Use Pickups[1]. Having a vocal line come in a couple of notes before the new section starts creates strong anticipation and can therefore be used to introduce tension.

Split Lines. A technique I learned from public speakers is splitting lines: Instead of taking a pause at the end of every sentence, they take their pauses half way through. This way, they can already think of what to say next, thus keeping the show going and at the same time they're creating tension - we all want to hear the thought brought to its completion. If we don't do this

See? You can use this technique for your songs, too. For example, split up the last line of your verse and finish it in the pre-chorus. So instead of going *"Girl, I don't get you"* try *"You know I (pause, new section) just don't get you"*. The longer the pause the stronger the tension[2].

Ouroboros Melodies. The ouroboros is an ancient symbol of a snake biting its own tail. You have probably never heard of this technique before and that is a) because I

---

1 Miley Cyrus - *Wrecking Ball (0:41)*, Justin Timberlake - *Cry Me A River (chorus)*, Ke$ha - *TiK ToK (chorus)*
2 Jhené Aiko - *The Worst (0:43)*

came up with the name and b) because it's extremely rare. So rare that I wouldn't have put it in this book, but this is just too awesome not to be shared. This is the kind of stuff that really gets me excited[1].

The idea is to move the lyrical blocks in relation to the music:

NORMALLY STRUCTURED MELODY.

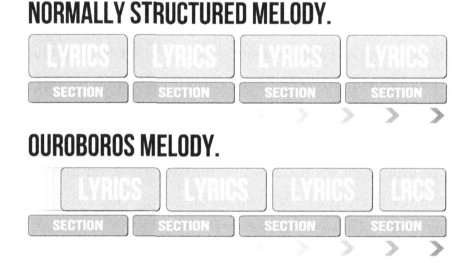

OUROBOROS MELODY.

The amazing thing about this technique is that your music and lyrics dovetail into each other, thereby working together to guide your listeners attention through the song[2]. Ouroboros Melodies. Give it a try.

---

1 That and Pretzel day.

2 Staind - *Failing (verse)*

IMPLY TENSION

Implied Tension in lyrics can again be divided into two parts, contentual and structural, and again structural implied tension is the stronger of the two as it can be felt regardless of whether your audience is listening to the lyrics or not.

CONTENTUAL IMPLIED TENSION

Tension can be implied by writing lyrics that contrast the music. This could mean either writing low-energy lyrics to a high-energy section or putting high-energy lyrics to a low-energy section.

Contrasting Low-Energy Music. Setting a big message against rather small music can be very powerful. This is often used in politically critical songs[1] (here, it sounds honest and brutally real) or when writing about violence or pain[2] (sounding detached).

---

1 Nena - *99 Luftballons,* A Perfect Circle - *Annihilation*

2 Pink - *Family Portrait,* Seether - *Given (verse),* Nirvana - *Rape Me (intro),* Papa Roach - *Broken Home (intro),* and many more very disturbing metal songs.

Contrasting High-Energy Music. This creates a disconnect feel from the music and can be used to imply boredom or apathy[1].

STRUCTURAL IMPLIED TENSION

Unbalanced Or Asymmetric Phrasal Structuring[2]. Going back to our 4-line blocks, realise that you don't have to write lyrics in blocks of 4 lines each. Try writing 3 or 5 lines per block and see what effect it has on the section.

The idea is to write more freely over a section, to break free from the tedious "one line every two bars" standard. Listen to the first verse of Zendaya's *Replay* where she uses this technique. Very cool, don't you think[3]?

Once you understand this technique, you will be able to look at a lyric sheet from across the room and still be able to tell whether it has this type of tension built into it. Let's try it right now: Which lyric has more tension?

---

1 Stromae - *Alors On Danse*

2 Perricone, J. - *Melody In Songwriting (Berklee Press, 2000)*

3 Clean Bandit - *Stronger (second verse)*, Rihanna - *Happy (chorus)*, Justin Timberlake - *Tunnel Vision (verses)*

Split Lines. A split line doesn't have to span two sections, it can also happen within a single section to imply tension. Again, the technique is to take pauses in the middle of your lines[1].

THE HOLLYWOOD STRUCTURE.

Now that we've looked at setting hype and tension, let's go through our hollywood structure and see what we can do specifically in every section:

The Intro. This is often instrumental, so there are rare-

---

1 Jhené Aiko - *The Worst (verses)*, Staind - *The Way I Am (chorus)*, Adele - *Someone Like You (first verse)*

ly any lyrics to be written for this section. You might however instruct the singer to improvise here (*"aw yeah yeah"*, *"you know what time it is"*, *"you ready?"*), although this seldomly contributes to your story. It does however tell us a little bit more about the mood that the song will be in and it introduces the vocals as soon as possible, which gives the audience something to hold on to.

The First Verse. Here we introduce our characters. Your first line is important (power position) - make sure to write something that grabs your audiences attention right away.

As we have learned, verses are generally a good moment for descriptions. The key is to really go into detail of what is going on. Nobody wants to hear that your girlfriend has the prettiest eyes. Tell us something specific, let us take a peek into your life - then and only then we might believe you[1].

I wrote a song once that started out with the lines:

---

1 Alex Clare - *Up All Night,* Lorde - *Royals,* Beyoncé - *Single Ladies*

I still make coffee for two
I'm not used to you not being around
I can't sleep at night because of you
but then again, might be the coffee, too.

See how that's much more interesting than "I miss you baby"? Verses. Get specific. Oh, and don't ever start a verse with "I've been walking through the streets/city" or "Woke up this morning". I will find you. It will not be pretty.

First Pre-Chorus. This will be just one or two lines that lead us nicely into the chorus. If you didn't already introduce your inciting incident in the first verse, then this is the moment.

First Chorus. Contrary to the verses, you want your chorus to be multi-faceted. The bigger the scope of possible interpretations, the better. No time for details here, this is big-picture stuff. So why is this important?

✓ It brings depth to your lyrics, thereby making your text 3-dimensional. And as we know from arranging, anything that makes your big sections bigger is invaluable for creating moments of gratification.

✓ The more ways your song can be interpreted, the more it will mean to different people. Take the line "You are gone" for example. It speaks to people who were dumped by their significant other, but it also reaches out to those who have recently experienced a death in their life[1].

✓ With multiple interpretations for your chorus you can actually set each of them up with your verses, thereby changing the meaning of the chorus every single time. This gives each chorus a unique, new color.

The Second Verse. Ah, yes. The time I have spent on second verses in my life. There was nothing I struggled with more than finding something new to say in verse 2. But as I found out through many years of trial-and-error, you actually have a lot of options here, and they all depend on what you did in the first verse. This makes it necessary to plan your lyrical structure before you start writing.

---

1 Just like "Left behind" speaks to people who have been deserted in the past and additionally satisfies the huge market of music enthusiasts with multiple asses.

- ✓ If you started telling a story in verse 1, keep going. Don't cram your entire trip to Nicaragua into one verse, take your time. Make us feel like we're there in verse 1, tell us what you did in verse 2.
- ✓ If you wrote about a certain problem, go deeper, tell us how it affects you and what it means to you. If your text is about how your significant other snores in their sleep, drill down in the second verse. You can't sleep, you get annoyed at them, you have a strained neck from sleeping on the couch - blow up the problem.
- ✓ Set up a new interpretation for the chorus. You have two options here:

Option 1 is to tell completely unrelated stories in the verses that introduce a new point of view to the main line:

> *Verse 1: The Petersons have a nice family lunch together and play board games together.*
>
> *Chorus: Oh Sunday, best of days.*

MEANING: WHAT A BEAUTIFUL DAY TO BE WITH YOUR FAMILY.

Verse 2: Mike Smith watches TV and drinks beer in his Superman underwear.

Chorus: Oh Sunday, best of days.

MEANING: WHAT A GREAT DAY TO DO NOTHING.

Option 2 is somewhat harder to pull off. It's about telling a continuous story:

Verse 1: Missed the bus to work, got splashed, went back home to change and realized I had no clean clothes.

Chorus: Life works in mysterious ways sometimes.

MEANING: IT SEEMS UNFAIR.

Verse 2: Went to buy a new shirt and ran into this beautiful woman who also had gotten splashed.

Chorus: Life works in mysterious ways sometimes.

MEANING: A BAD THING CAN TURN OUT TO BE A GOOD THING IN HINDSIGHT.

In both cases, the process is to think of a multi-faceted line for the chorus first, then see how you can setup different ways of leading into it to allow for these different interpretations.

It's often a good technique to zoom out for the second verse. Go from the mundane to the magnificent, from one person to the world, from experience to lessons learned. This way, you establish the second verse as higher in energy than the first.

The Second Pre-Chorus. This may be the same as pre-chorus 1 or it may be different - your choice. The same rules apply.

The Second Chorus. Usually, choruses 1, 2 and 3 have the same lyrics. You can change them if you want to, but you are losing your repetition. And we like repetition. And we like repetition. As we have seen in this chapter, just because all the choruses have the same lyrics does *not* mean that they also all represent the same message.

The Prim. Bridge. You can see the primary bridge as a way of continuing your story from before or you follow the energy curve and introduce an element of surprise here.

This can be anything from changing your writing technique (e.g. by going from sung lyrics to rapping)[1] to turning the whole situation around (the "Sixth Sense" approach)[2]. As always, the prim. bridge is a good moment to get creative.

The Third Chorus. The same goes as for Chorus #2.

The Fourth Chorus. As already discussed earlier, you can change the lyrics here if you want. Use them to really drive your point home.

Ending. Depending on what you're doing, you have the option of adding some lyrics here. If you're going back to the beginning musically, do the same with the lyrics.

If you're ending on a high energy level, make sure the lyrics reflect that. If you're cutting out of the song rath-

---

1 Katy Perry - Dark Horse (feat. Juicy J), Justin Bieber - Beauty And A Beat (feat. Nikki Minaj)
2 Beyoncé - Single Ladies, If I Were A Boy

er abruptly, think about bringing this idea back lyrically.

If you're fading out your song, consider ending on free lyrics ("yeah"s or slight alterations of your chorus).

SUMMARY:

✓ Power positions are certain moments in your song that give whatever lyrical line is there a lot of power.

✓ Hype can be controlled with scope and power words.

✓ Tension can be applied with contentual tension (by telling a story or using cliffhangers) or structural tension (pickups, split lines and ouroboros melodies).

✓ Tension can be implied contentually (setting low energy lyrics against high energy music and vice-versa) and structurally (using unbalanced or asymmetric phrasal structuring or split lines).

✓ Keep your verses specific and detailed, go big-picture and multidimensional in your choruses.

PRODUCTION

Production is huge and it's getting bigger and bigger. As a modern songwriter you absolutely have to be able to produce your own stuff, even if it's just for demo purposes. This is not just a commodity anymore. You can't sell sheet music. There is a certain standard for how your music has to sound and if you don't deliver you don't stand a chance.

So I think we have to make an important distinction here as that term "music production" has come to mean so many different things. We will not be talking about mixing or mastering technique here. The music production I will be talking about in this book is a creative one - using effects and sound design to tell your story and ride the energy curve.

Music production is finding its way into songwriting. We have entered an era of *sound design,* to a degree that most new songwriters these days know more about compression than arrangement. The old songwriting rule "It's not a good song if it won't work on piano" no longer applies. Just think of rap, metal or dance music. The writing and the whole production process have become one.

In this chapter, we will look at how production can be used creatively to help us ride our energy curve.

SETTING HYPE

Production as a tool for setting hype ranges from extremely subtle techniques to major changes in sound. I want you to see the following techniques in the same way as when we looked at different vocal modes or guitar playing styles. Do this and you will see that creative production really isn't that different from all the other songwriting elements and that you already know most of the techniques in some shape or form. So here they are:

FATTENING / THINNING OUT.

This includes *Layering, Compression, Filter, Chorus* and *Distortion*. It's simple, really: The thicker your instrument, the higher the hype and vice versa. Layering and compression are similar to doubling a part, filters can be compared to thinning out our texture through arrangement and distortion we have already discussed when we talked about vocals, bass and guitar effects.

PERCEIVED VOLUME.

I'm refering to *Compression* and *Volume Automation*. Hype - as we have learned when we talked about parts - can be controlled by volume. For example, pulling down your verses a couple of decibel (thus decreasing its hype level) gives your chorus some additional lift.

DIMENSION / SPACE.

This includes *Stereo Enhancing Effects, Reverb* and *Delay*[1]. Dimension is interesting as really there was no way before music production to use it as a means to control hype. The rule is this: The wider an instrument is spread and the closer it is to the listener, the higher its

---

1 Leona Lewis - *Bleeding Love (getting wider & deeper at 0:56)*

hype level will be. Reverb is slowly making its way back into mainstream as I write this, but part of the reason it was "out" for a while is because it lowers hype considerably.

Remember that space is relative, so if all your instruments are dry your mix will still sound low in hype - you need some wet instruments in the back to make your dry instruments jump forward. Similarly, if your entire song is wide, your chorus won't stand out as much.

NEW INSTRUMENTS.

You could add new instruments such as *Pads, Percussion, Synths* and *Samples*. You might actually completely change the arrangement by adding new instruments and thus enlarging the texture. This of course leads to an increase in hype. Be careful about this technique: I have found myself more than once adding instruments to a verse to make it sound better (as in: fuller, prettier) while forgetting that as a side product, I was also increasing hype. The result was that my chorus sounded tiny in comparison. So always listen to your enriched section in context - can you still hear the energy curve?

PROCESSING.

Any effect can increase hype if applied noticeably. This includes glitchy effects as in the intro to OutKast's *Ms. Jackson*, distortion like in the bridge to Taylor Swift's *Shake It Off*, delays as on the guitar in U2's *Where The Streets Have No Name*, low pass filters modulated by an LFO (wobble) as on the bass in Alex Clare's *Too Close*, tremolos as in the verse to Audioslaves *Gasoline*, side chaining and on and on and on. As you can see, most of these techniques bring the subdivision of the instrument to a higher level, which results in an increase of hype.

USING TENSION

Production is used excessively to introduce tension to music. This can go from barely noticeable to very obvious and everything in between - all the fine tuning is under your control. There are two important ways of introducing tension: *Automation* and *Sound Effects (SFX)*.

AUTOMATION.

All the effects above can be automated to introduce tension to a mix:

Fattening / Thinning Out[1]. For this technique, additional layers are slowly faded in, the threshold of a compressor is gradually increased to let more punch through, the cut-off frequency of a filter is automated or the wet/dry knob of your favorite distortion or chorus plugin is slowly opened up.

Perceived Volume[2]. By slowly increasing the volume of an instrument, the producer is mimicking a crescendo, which as we know introduces tension. For the first time in history, volume automation allows us to crescendo any instrument we want, even instruments that normally aren't able to do that, such as the organ.

Dimension / Space[3]. Tension can be introduced by automating the dry/wet knob of your reverb or delay or by changing the wideness of your stereo enhancer. This

---

1 Ariana Grande - *Break Free (feat. Zedd, filter the synth in the verse),* Jhené Aiko - *It's Cool (keep listening to the filter on the snare drum coming in at 0:56),* Katy Perry - *Roar (main vocals are doubled at 0:54),* Maroon 5 - *Moves Like Jagger (filter on guitars in verse & snare at 1:32)*
2 Massive Attack - *Angel (bass gets louder at 0:51),* Mudvayne - *Cradle (the vocals are pulled down at 0:33 to give the next section more impact)*
3 Carly Rae Jepsen - *Call Me Maybe (getting wider & deeper at 0:24),* LMFAO - *Party Rock Anthem (automated reverb at 2:16)*

adds another dimension to your mix and opens everything up.

New Instruments[1]. By bringing in instruments half way through a section, you are again affecting the arrangement.

Processing[2]. Gradually changing an instrument's sound can be used to introduce tension. This may remind you of the chapter on vocal effects, where we looked at how singers can increase tension by changing their vocal mode or by slowly adding twang to their voice. Processing is the exact same thing! Think of a new set of effects you can use to communicate to your listener how your singer feels.

SOUND EFFECTS.

This includes *Swooshes, Sweeps, Uplifters, Downlifters* and *Reverses*[3].

---

1 Evanescence - *Bring Me To Life (guitar at 0:28)*, Clean Bandit - *Rather Be (feat. Jess Glynne, hi hat 0:40 - 0:48)*
2 Massive Attack - *Angel (bass 1:05 - 1:34 and back to 1:46)*
3 Katy Perry - *Firework (uplifter at 1:01 - 1:17)*, Gnarls Barkley - *Crazy (side-chained uplifter at 0:33)*, Carly Rae Jepsen - *Call Me Maybe...*

Although it doesn't feel like it in the production process, this is actually just another sub-point of automation since most of these are just white noise going through an automated filter. All of these can be used to control tension, whether positively (swooshes, sweeps, uplifters) or negatively (downlifters).

It makes sense to start collecting different sound effects for your songs in a special folder that you can drag & drop into your sessions.

Because production is the element which you have the most control over, it lends itself particularly well for subtle manoeuvres like this.

I want to share three of my favorite techniques here to give you an idea of what is possible with production.

(uplifter at 0:24, piano reverse at 1:00), Maroon 5 - *Moves Like Jagger* *(downlifter at 1:11)*

LOW & HIGH PASS FILTERS.

By noticeably cutting off the low or high end of an essential element to your mix, you are audibly thinning out the arrangement, which results in the desired implied tension[1].

AUTO-FILTERS.

Since filtering always has an aftertaste of tension, using auto-filters on an instrument can also be used to create implied tension. The direction of the cut off isn't important here, the important bit is that we can hear that there is some filtering happening[2].

VOCAL PROCESSING.

It is possible to imply tension on the vocals through effects, such as compression, certain kinds of reverb, delays or auto-tune. These are all very subtle, but the tension comes from the fact that we subconsciously notice the difference between what we hear and what we know a voice is supposed to sound like[3].

---

1 Kid Cudi Vs Crookers - *'Day 'N' Nite' (Radio Edit, drum loop at 0:37 - 0:51)*

2 Iggy Azalea - *Fancy (hi hat pattern at 0:31)*

3 Drake - *Started From The Bottom (auto-tune, compression)*, Ace Hood...

SUMMARY:

✓ Hype can be altered by fattening or thinning out (layering, compression, filters, chorus and distortion), by using dimension / space (stereo enhancing plugins, reverb, delay), new instruments (pads, percussion, synths, samples) or processing.

✓ Tension can be applied by automating all the above or by using sound effects.

✓ Implied tension can be achieved through the use of high pass filters, auto filters and vocal processing.

- Bugatti (feat. Future, Rick Ross, auto-tune, compression, delay)

END OF PART II

That wraps up our elements. Glad you're still with me.

Before we move to part III, there is something we need to discuss. Even though you might think you've learned a lot from this book already, you really haven't learned a thing until you've used what you learned. To put it bluntly: *Knowing* something isn't worth shit.

This book will be useless to you if you don't set yourself clear goals of using the techniques you have learned in this book. Start with three new techniques in every song you write from now on. Otherwise you will get stuck where you are right now for the rest of your life. That's just how our brain operates: We don't remember anything unless we hear it repeatedly.

So I suggest going through all the techniques again and highlighting anything you haven't used before. And then try 'em out! Even if you don't like the example songs showcasing the technique, figure out a way of making them work for you. You could be the first to ever use one of these in a completely new way.

After learning about all of these techniques, now it's time for you to come up with some of your own. In part 3, we will look at how to create new techniques you can use in your songs today (this is the only song-writing book in the world that teaches this). Having a unique set of writing tools is a huge, huge step in the direction of a sound that stands out. The techniques in this book are really just the beginning. Can you write a hit song with what you've learned so far? Absolutely. But if you want to take your songwriting to a whole new level then you will find the skill to create your own techniques on the spot invaluable.

We round of part 3 of this book with my "Moving Boreders" concept, which is my favorite test to see if my song is doing its job and a 10-step formula to writing an addictive song.

PART 3: APPLICATION

In this part you will learn:

✓ The exact steps of writing a addictive song.

✓ How to become a more original writer

✓ How to figure out if there's a problematic section in your song you might need to rewrite.

✓ Where to go from here

YOUR OWN TECHNIQUES IN 4 SIMPLE STEPS

Without any further ado, here's how to create your own unique set of tools you can use forever and ever in four simple steps:

STEP 1

Know which kind of compartment you are looking for. I like to think of my set of techniques as tools in a tool box. There are six compartments (arrangement, harmony, rhythm, parts, lyrics and production), all of which are divided into three more sub-compartments (hype, tension and implied tension).

For the sake of this discussion, let's decide that we're looking for a technique in the part-writing/tension compartment.

STEP 2

Know what your technique needs to be able to do. In our example, we are interested in tension, so the concept is to lead the audience from one hype level to another.

STEP 3.1

Translate your technique from another compartment. If you are looking for a hype technique, try to remove the time element of a tension technique.

Vice versa, when looking for tension, try to add a time element to a hype technique. And when looking for an implied tension technique, see how you could use the tensest moment from a tension technique throughout a whole section.

So I'm looking for a tension technique in the part-writing compartment, meaning I start by looking at the hype techniques. The most important ones that recur in every instrument are: Dynamics, Range, Modes, Effects and Variety.

If we add a time element to these 5 techniques, we get Crescendos, Ascending Melodies, Changing the Vocal Mode, Creating Tension with Effects, and…? It seems that we have found something:

Variety doesn't have a tension-counterpart yet.

STEP 3.2

If you can't find a counterpart in any of the techniques given in this book, try to come up with one on your own! For example, you could try to find more techniques for negative tension to get your transitions from chorus to verse under control. Or you start by going through every plugin in your DAW to see how you could use them to tell your story: Find out how they influence hype and see what you can automate to create tension. Think out of the box here. If you're making a music video for your song, think of visual ways to tell your story. Or consider your live performances: What could you do to display your song's energy curve through your facial expressions, body language or light show?

STEP 4

Now, all that's left to do is find a technique that fits your description. So we need a time-based version of variety or in other words, the idea is to change the level of variety throughout a section. Since we want to move up in energy, how about a one-note melody that turns into something a bit more melodic in the second half of the section[1]? You get the idea.

---

1 Meghan Trainor - *All About That Bass (0:38 - 0:45)*

So, right now, go to your computer and start a new word document. Call it "The Toolbox". Divide it into the compartments arrangement, harmony, rhythm, part-writing, lyrics and production and subdivide with hype, tension and implied tension. Add more elements like light show, music video or body language if you like and subdivide these as well. Then start filling your personalized tool box with techniques. You can start with the ones from this book here, but make sure you expand it with some original ones as well.

And lastly, if you find a great technique, send me an email, I would love to know about it (you can find my email at the end of this book)!

SUMMARY:

✓ Know which kind of compartment you are looking for.
✓ Know what your technique needs to be able to do.
✓ Translate your technique from another compartment or try to come up with one on your own.
✓ Find a technique that fits your description.

(S)HIT TEST #2: MOVING BOREDERS
Does Your Song Do Its Job?

In this chapter I want to share with you my favorite tool for analyzing songs to identify problematic sections. I call this "moving boreders":

The idea is to listen to your finished song (preferably after a day or two) and pretending you have never heard it before. Getting in this state of mind can be challenging but is necessary for using this technique. It helps to bounce your track and listen to it in a new context. For example, you could put it in an iTunes playlist of comparable hit songs. I like to go for a little walk and listen to it on my iPod. It really doesn't matter what you do, as long as you can recreate that feeling of hearing a song for the very first time.

Once you are in this state, you are ready to take the next step: Identifying the bored-line. The bored-line is the moment in your song when your audience changes the station, when they feel like they have heard what they needed to hear. In a bad song, this is often around the 15 second mark (when the vocals come in). If I had to guess from experience, I'd say that your average is probably around 1:15 (when the second verse hits).

The bored-line is your biggest enemy when it comes to storytelling. Just think how many listeners are never gonna hear your fantastic finale because they turned off your song during the second verse or in the bridge. And attention-spans for songs are getting shorter and shorter.

Your bored-line occurs at the moment in your song when…

➤ You're not giving your audience enough reasons to keep listening.
➤ They don't like an element in your song (style, vocals and production are the biggest culprits here).
➤ Your listener is confused. This generally means they can't follow the story.

These are the three biggest mistakes I hear writers make - even professionals do it. Note that none of these happen consciously - so you can't just go out and ask people what they think of your song. If you do that, people will listen because you're forcing them to. If they like your finale they will like your song. But that's not what is important - because if the rest of your song sucks they never would've gotten there if you hadn't asked them to listen to the whole thing.

We talked about having a friend draw your energy curve and that's the best way to go if you haven't released yet. But if your song is already out there, track how well it's doing. You can check the average time people listen to your songs on youtube using the site's analytics tool. This might just be the easiest way of figuring out where your bored-line is.

Once you've identified your bored-line, move it back further and further. The best scenario is obviously if you can move it past the ending of your song. All the techniques you have learned in this book can help you in achieving this goal. Play with different levels of hype and increase tension when you feel like you're losing your audience's attention.

Another way of moving the bored-line is to shorten your song. This is known as "killing your babies" and is always a difficult step for a writer although it is usually the best solution. Consider this especially if your song is longer than 4 minutes. The feedback I give the most frequently to writers is to shorten either their second verse or the bridge. So don't push it. Watch how people react to your song and act accordingly.

SUMMARY:

✓ Put yourself into a state of hearing your song for the very first time.

✓ Identify your bored-line.

✓ Move back your bored-line as much as you can.

THE ADDICTION FORMULA IN 10 SIMPLE STEPS

Now that we have all the techniques we need, let's go through the process of writing a complete song with the Addiction Formula from start to finish.

1) WRITE A SECTION.

Don't think, just write. The easiest way for me to come up with something is to just sit with my guitar or piano and play, play, play. Play some chords, find a good melody, go back and forth until the two form a unit. Go into your sequencer and start a new session. Record your vocals to a click, then add other instruments to taste.

2) DETERMINE WHAT YOU HAVE.

Now begins the judging process. Listen to your section and feel out what kind of section it is - is it a chorus, verse, bridge, intro or riff? Make your decision depending on what you learned about each section in *"Hollywood's Secret Formula - The Most Popular Form In The World"*.

3) FIND YOUR ENERGY CURVE.

Next, you want to figure out a compelling story to tell. Follow the steps we have learned in *"The Perfect Energy Curve - Let's Go For A Ride"* to make an image in your mind of what your song's energy curve looks like. Grab a sheet of paper and commit to a curve. You can copy the blueprints for my coordinate system at the end of the book if you like or just sketch it out yourself. Write the section's names below the x-axis.

4) MAKE A ROUGH OUTLINE.

Open up your sequencer and set markers for each section of your song (start with 8 bars each). Now copy/paste what you have to its respective positions in the song. Write the other sections, making sure that they roughly follow the specifications we have learned in *"And... Scene! - Let's Write A Thriller"*.

5) SET HYPE LEVELS

If you've done a good job writing your sections, this will make this step much quicker. Consult your energy curve and make sure that each section has the the proper amount of energy. Use whatever technique you want from part II of this book to set those hype levels. Strip out instruments if necessary.

6) INTRODUCE TENSION

Now it's time to take care of all the transitions. So go through your song again and introduce tension where your curve tells you to. With this book, you have a long list of techniques you can use to accomplish this. Rewrite sections if necessary.

7) PLAY WITH IMPLIED TENSION

By now you should have a near-finished song. But before you finish it off, go through it once more and mute tracks here and there to see what effect it has on the music. See if you can create some implied tension this way. Even if your section goes way down in hype after muting an instrument it might still work. Remember, Katy Perry's *Firework* goes way down in its pre-chorus and it still works out great.

8) (S)HIT TEST #1: THE FRIEND TEST

Next, send out your song to a friend of yours as described in *"The Perfect Energy Curve - Let's Go For A Ride"*. I suggest sending it to various people (including non-musicians) to see what they think. If you get feedback, see if you agree (after shaking off the initial "they just don't get how special my music is!"). And if you do agree (and believe me, your friends are never wrong!), go back into your session and rewrite the critical bits.

9) (S)HIT TEST #2: MOVING BOREDERS

After you've finished your production, let your song rest a day or two if possible. Then come back to it with a fresh set of ears and identify its bored-line as described in *"Moving Boreders - Does Your Song Do Its Job?"*. Make sure you move it back as far as you can.

10) RELEASE.

Whole books have been written just about this process, but I won't go into this here. Just a couple of tips: As I said in *"Moving Boreders - Does Your Song Do Its Job?"*, use youtube analytics to figure out problem zones in your music, collect feedback from comments and rewrite if you feel like you can significantly improve your song. But mostly, learn from your feedback for future songs. Figure out what didn't work and why. This is your best teacher, because it is tailored specifically to your style - don't miss out on this step!

Want a more detailed explanation? Go to holistic-songwriting.com/7dayhitsongprogram, where you can get a 7 day audio program that takes you through all the steps of writing a song for just $7 (a dollar a day).

SUMMARY:

✓ Write a section.

✓ Determine what you have.

✓ Find your energy curve.

✓ Make a rough outline.

✓ Set hype levels.

✓ Introduce tension.

✓ Play with implied tension.

✓ Shit test #1: Moving boreders.

✓ Shit test #2: Have a friend draw your energy curve.

✓ Release.

EPILOGUE

I started writing this book 10 years ago when I was just a teenager. Looking through old notes on what to include in this book I realized that what I've always been looking for in my career as a songwriter was a sense of knowing why we do what we do.

When I discovered the 3 act structure in music, that opened up a new world for me. I realized that beauty has universal rules. I began looking for the structure in other parts of my life - public speaking, card magic, marketing, psychology - and have found it time and time again. And each time I discover it in a new discipline, it redefines music for me.

Most of the insights in this book I discovered because of my fascination for the psychology of performing arts. What are the subliminal triggers that make me enjoy one magic performance more than another? Why did I buy this book and lost interest in another? Why did this workshop go better than the last?

I used to get frustrated over people who didn't understand my music. What were they thinking? Were they even paying attention? I had some really great stories to tell, always had an innovative concept. But people still didn't listen. When I showed off my songs, they talked through them.

It took me a while to figure out what was going on: I had forgotten that thinking of a story is just the first part. The part that resonates with people, that sticks with them, is how your story is told. If you can't communicate your idea through your music (and you can tell this is the case if you start your pitches with "so the idea behind this song is this…"), no one cares how ground-breaking your story is. It's the equivalent of listening to a public speaker with a stutter: He might have the greatest content in the world, but if we get distracted by his way of talking, we drift off.

When I discovered the Addiction Formula, it completely changed my game. The first song I ever wrote that used it immediately won a contest and I've since won many pitches with it. It has been my secret weapon for over 6 years now and I sincerely hope you can use it for your songs. Good luck!

THANK YOU!

Thank you for reading *The Addiction Formula*. It has been a pleasure writing this book and it is the first time I have shared some of my best-kept secrets with a public audience. But really, this book is just the beginning.

If you want to go deeper with the Addiction Formula or if you're interested in my Inner Game or Business products, head on over to my website (holistic-songwriting.com), where you can find all my newest releases.

You get my best stuff by following my newsletter or by subscribing to the facebook and twitter pages:
facebook.com/holisticsongwriting
twitter.com/HolisticSongs

If you have any requests for future products, questions, comments or a success story you would like to share I would love to hear those as well - give me the good and bad!

Drop me an email at:
me@holistic-songwriting.com

ACKNOWLEDGEMENTS

I would like to thank Ulrike, Havo, Joanna and Philip for making me feel less crazy about my own life by leading crazy lives yourselves. This book is dedicated to you.

Thomas, Julius and Carlos for being there for me through thick, medium and thin.

Tom Salisbury and Benjamin Samama for their feedback to the first draft of this book. I think I changed about 90% of the original book and that's a good thing - thank you!

Florian Enderle for lighting a spark inside of me that has ultimately lead me to the discovery of the Addiction Formula. Stay gefährlich, Florian.

Erwin Steijlen, Conrad Pope, Imogen Heap, Jeff Rona, Nathan Rightnour, Bernhard Hoffmann, Zeus Held and Peter Leutscher-Kintrup for surprising me with overwhelming support and kindness when I didn't expect it.

James, Sebastian and Lorenz - my first band. Working with you guys taught me all I know, and not just about songwriting.

And last but not least, I would like to thank Yasmin Kurth for continuously pushing me towards writing this book. Jazz, this wouldn't have happened without you.

ABOUT THE AUTHOR

After spending some time at International Music College Freiburg, Friedemann realized that he had made a mistake studying jazz guitar. For two years he had spent every day trying to improve his playing technique - with no success. Rehearsing scales was not his thing. Instead, under the radar of his teachers, Friedemann wrote songs.

When he barely made his final guitar exam and his composition teacher (and creative director of the school) Bernhard G. Hoffmann heard his songs and told him "There is nothing more I can teach you", Friedemann quit the program and moved to the Netherlands.

Here, he studied MediaMusic and his songwriting exploded. In the following four years, Friedemann played in front of over a 100,000 people with his band, conducted his music in front of a live orchestra, was featured on prime time television, won two composition awards, had his music going to Cannes Film Festival and worked for some of the biggest names in the industry, incl. Ubisoft, ADT Security and Apple. He has received recommendations from songwriters Erwin Steijlen (Pink, Shakira) and René Merkelbach (Within Temptation), orchestrator Conrad Pope (The Hobbit, Harry Potter) and composer Jeff Rona (Traffic, God Of War III).

This is his first book.

ENERGY CURVE BLUEPRINT

MAX ← ENERGY LEVEL → MIN

TOOLBOX

You can use this page to kick-start
your tool-box of original techniques

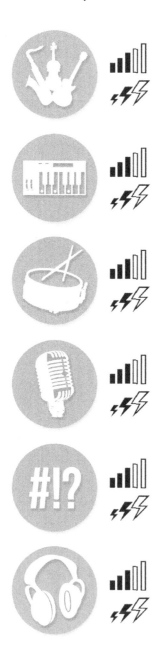

GLOSSARY

1-2-3 Rule: *When in doubt where to start a new section, follow this rule: 1 Introduce, 2 Repeat, 3 Change.*

Addiction Formula, the: *A holistic approach to writing songs in which energy rules and organizes all of the elements. Designed to keep the audience hooked and alert.*

Bored-line: *The moment of your song where your audience loses interest and changes the station. The songwriters goal is to move this moment as far back as possible.*

Element: *An integral part of the songwriting process. The six elements of songwriting are: Arrangement, Harmony, Rhythm, Part-Writing, Lyrics and Production.*

Energy: *Consisting of hype and tension, energy is the guiding principle behind the the Addiction Formula. Energy is a relative term that can only be measured in context.*

Gefährlich [g'fair‚lish]: *German for "dangerous". Referring to a way of writing that is set out to captivate the listener.*

Hollywood Structure: *Based on the 3-act structure of film, this describes a song with 3 points of gratification, typically arranged in the following way: Intro, verse, verse cont., pre-chorus, chorus, (interlude,) verse, pre-chorus, chorus, prim. bridge, prim. bridge cont., chorus, finale, (outro.)*

Hype: *A relative energy level that is stationary. Ideally, it jumps with the beginning of a new section.*

Implied Tension: *A kind of tension that relies on noticeably subtracting parts from the song's arrangement. This creates a hole in the music which wants to be filled and therefore gives the section in question direction.*

Lyric-Less Storytelling: *The art of expressing a story through music, and not necessarily through lyrics.*

Negative Tension: *Negative tension is a kind of tension in which the energy level of a section is brought down smoothly. It is not widely used in pop music, as generally we want our audience's excitement to go up, not down. Examples are downlifters, descending melodies, ending a progression on the tonic and drum fills in a low subdivision.*

Power Positions: *These are the moments of greatest change in your songs. Placing a great lyric here is wildly effective.*

Section: *A section is a part of your song that is either 4 (in slow tempos), 8 or 16 measures long. A pre-chorus is a section, or a verse.*

Shit-Test: *The two shit-tests in this book can be used to figure out if your song is doing its job. The two shit-tests presented are the "Friend Test" and the "Moving Boreders" test.*

Story: *A succession of moments of gratification and periods of anticipation.*

Structure: *This refers to how your sections follow one another, for example into, verse, chorus, verse, chorus, outro. The most popular structure in the world is the hollywood structure.*

Sub1, Sub2, Sub4, Sub8, Sub16, Sub32: *This refers to subdivisions. A sub4 is a subdivision of a measure which divides it into 4 equal parts. By adding 8th notes to that pattern, the subdivision is brought up to sub8.*

Tension: *A tool for smoothing out jumps in hype. Tension is always moving somewhere (typically up).*

Made in the USA
Monee, IL
28 March 2023

30735778R00128